CHANGE YOUR MIND,
CHANGE YOUR LIFE

CHANGE YOUR MIND, CHANGE YOUR LIFE

A book to help you change what does not work for you in your life, to what will.

Leon Norell

ISBN 0-9544616-0-6

Typeset by Tradespools, Chippenham, Wiltshire
Printed by Antony Rowe Ltd, Eastbourne, East Sussex

The purpose of life is to change.
Change is the reason for being born.

A traveller arrived in town. 'Tell me,' he enquired of one of the inhabitants, 'how are the people in this town?'. 'How are they where you come from,' the inhabitant asked. 'Oh, not too friendly,' the man responded. 'Well you'll find them much like that here, too,' the inhabitant replied.

Shortly afterwards another traveller arrived. 'Tell me,' he enquired of the inhabitant, 'how are the people in this town?' 'How are they where you come from?' the inhabitant asked. 'Oh, very friendly,' said the traveller. 'Well,' replied the inhabitant, 'you'll find them much like that here, too.'

Our planet may be regarded as consisting of many worlds, which vary according to the intentions of those who inhabit them. One of those worlds is inhabited by people who regard it as a jungle and their personal interests as paramount. Another is inhabited by those who regard it as a place where everyone respects one another toward their mutual advancement. Which world is yours?

One of the greatest problems that we encounter in our lives, is doing what is inconsistent with our true nature, or following directions in life that we later regret. Yet some of the greatest people throughout history — indeed in the world today — have passed the earlier parts of their lives in this way, later to change direction and complete their lives doing what was *consistent* with their true nature, or that was for the highest good of the world.

DEDICATION

When I was eight, I ran away from my boarding school, in Sussex, England. On reaching the railway station I found I did not have the seven shillings and six pence I needed for my fare home to London.

I approached a man and asked him if he would lend me the money, but he said no. I asked a woman. She said no, too. I began to panic. My heart was pounding, the train was about to leave and I knew the school authorities would be coming after me.

Then my eye was drawn to a tall man. I think he was an American. I explained that my train was about to leave and that I needed seven shillings and sixpence to get to London. Without hesitating, the man took a ten-shilling note from his wallet and handed it to me. I said I would return with the change, but he just smiled and, placing his hand on my shoulder, he said: 'That's all right'.

I dedicate this book to that man and to all in the world who are there when others need them. I also dedicate this book to Freda Dodd, now in the spiritual dimension, who opened my eyes to that dimension many years ago; and to my parents, also in that dimension, who provided me with this lifetime.

CONTENTS

ACKNOWLEDGEMENTS

Throughout the twenty-five years during which I have worked on this book, many people have helped or inspired me in their individual ways. I have read various books and articles, attended personal growth seminars and talked to people from different walks of life and spiritual dimensions. Inspirations from all these sources have found their way into this book. To my regret, I cannot identify all of those sources, to give them their deserved credits. For all their inspirations and contributions, however, I am grateful.

I would like to express particular gratitude to my friend Keith Wakelam, author of *The Individual Universe* and *Understanding Eternity* for his advice, to the facilitators of *Insight Seminars*, whose patience helped me resolve some of my problematic life-issues and to the many friends and business acquaintances who, though they were unaware of it, were there just when I needed them.

THE MIND IS LIKE A PARACHUTE –
IT WORKS BEST OPEN

Russell Bishop

ABOUT THIS BOOK

I am not a psychologist, nor do I have any qualifications in that field. I am an Oriental rug dealer, with my fair share of life-experience.

I was born in London in 1937, the youngest of four. Soon after the outbreak of war, our father moved us to the relative safety of the English countryside by the sea, in Torquay, Devon. My parents, Iranian Jews, gained British citizenship in 1933; a privilege they always respected. My father, a wheat farmer in the beautiful hills overlooking Teheran, came to England with little money, to become an internationally known rug merchant in the years to follow. Inwardly yearning to be loved, he was 'head of the house' and we addressed him accordingly. My mother was the one with whom we would talk.

At the age of eight, emotionally unsettled by my parents' incompatibility, I was sent, on the recommendation of a psychiatrist, to a boarding school in Sussex. In contrast to my mother's cosseting, this was to be one of the most traumatic experiences of my life … and running away, as I was soon to discover, a *severely* punishable offence.

I left the last of my various schools at sixteen, with little academic accomplishment of which to boast. With not the faintest idea of how to behave toward those of the opposite sex, I compensated for my feelings of inadequacy by cultivating an overconfident front, in a hopeless attempt to impress them into admiring me. My perspectives, warped — or should I say *mangled* — by films of the fifties, depicting lovelorn females swooning into their arms, I tried imitating the slick and swaggering role models of the time. All to no avail. Eventually, the pain of rejection and fear of further rejection was so terrible that, to survive emotionally, I closed down the finer aspects of my nature. The way to succeed with women, I determined in later years, was not through warmth or sensitivity, but through a cold and detached demeanour; one that, to my regret, I adopted. 'I love you,' were not words I would say.

Glimmerings of higher things

It was while in the RAF, at twenty, that I met an amazing woman called Freda Dodd, introduced to me by her daughter Anne, whom I met at a dance one evening. A highly evolved 'spiritual' clairvoyant and one of the most significant people to figure in my life, Freda took me under her wing. Through her I came to see that we are not our bodies, nor our brains, but intelligences (generally referred to as 'spirits', or 'souls') attached for limited periods to the bodies we possess and that anchor us to this planet. What we refer to as 'death', I learned, is the moment at which our bodies can no longer sustain us here, whereupon we continue our existences in some non-physical, or 'spiritual' dimension.

Freda spoke of the 'spiritual people' in non-physical dimensions, whom she could see and with whom she could actually converse, as readily as with those in this physical dimension. She spoke of the energies, colours, beauty and life in those dimensions, which one would never imagine existed. That chance meeting (or was it chance?) was to prove one of the most important milestones in my life.

As a result of this introduction to life in other dimensions, I became increasingly conscious of the fact that our physical lives are not chance events, but that they have some purpose. Aside from any useful contributions we might also make to the planet, that purpose for each of us appears to be to refine the various aspects of our nature, cultivating 'higher' patterns of behaviour and eliminating any 'lower' ones we possess. The degrees to which we accomplish this, seemingly, determine the levels of existence into which we later find ourselves, when we 'die'.

To help us in the task of refining our natures, Freda explained, we can request the guidance of those in higher dimensions, to counsel us as far as we permit this, through their inspiration. I failed fully to appreciate the value of this information at the time and the next twenty-two years of my life were a shambles. I devoted much of my energy to searching for 'love', yet had relationships in which I seldom felt able to reciprocate, fully, the love that was shown to me. I was in constant conflict with my parents — particularly my father — and took irresponsible risks in business, as I now see it, to prove my worth. I underwent several years' daily psychoanalysis to free myself from my *excruciating* emotional turmoil and sustained two betrayals in business that culminated in bankruptcy and one of the darkest periods of my life. What had once been a good natured child was now an embittered young man, harbouring within him, an unappeasable determination for revenge.

My personal growth begins

At age forty, still in turmoil, I happened to attend an introductory talk by a young woman called Arianna Stassinopoulos, regarding a personal growth course presented by the world-wide organisation 'Insight Seminars'. Though highly suspicious, I attended the course. This was to prove another significant milestone in my life. Facilitated by people of integrity, with no religious agenda or personal interest, other than for the wellbeing of others, that course presented me with fresh perspectives on life. I came to see how, in very subtle ways, I had been sabotaging myself and penalising those about me, particularly women, for my earlier unhappy experiences. I also saw how I had been the author of much of my misfortune.

This brought me to the realisation that so much pain and disappointment in our lives could be avoided. It was just a matter of recognising the emotional mechanisms that drive us, letting go of the self-destructive and sometimes *absurd* beliefs we hold about ourselves, other people and the world — all holding us down, like weights around our feet — and seeing that there is some purpose to life, if we are only willing to recognise this.

Through these fresh perspectives, I began changing some of my counter-productive patterns and cultivating productive ones. I found myself becoming increasingly sensitive to others and understanding them more readily … even my adversaries! I wondered how it was that some people took delight in feeding pigeons in the park, while others took equal delight in running them down on the road. I wondered how elderly people I passed in the street might have been as children, starting out their lives, to become the pioneers of the world we now inherit; and how little honour they receive for their contributions to the world, which we take so much for granted.

Gradually, I let down my emotional guard. I allowed myself to love in a more genuine way and to give expression to the finer qualities I had been suppressing in earlier years. My father and I grew closer than we had ever been before. A new being was emerging in me ... one I much preferred.

The point of this book

Much of what you read here will not be new to you and much, no doubt, will not even remotely apply to you. However, it is offered not so much to 'inform' you, as to encourage you to focus your awareness on aspects of your nature that may not have occurred to you, yet that are working for and against your best interests. With that awareness, you can work at enhancing or neutralising them as you consider appropriate and, through focusing on the higher aspects of your nature, achieve greater success in your fields of endeavour, your relationships and your life.

I do not present myself as a model of perfection. I still have inner struggles and at times feel guilty, disappointed and angry. But that's what being 'human' is about; and changing as much as we can in the time we have available to us in this lifetime is, I believe, what 'life' is about.

What you will find in this book

In this book, therefore, I hope to show you what my own sometimes difficult life-experiences have shown me. These are that you are the author of some of your own fortunes and misfortunes; that until you alter your counter-productive and sometimes *misguided* patterns of behaviour, you will attract the same kinds of problem, disappointment or failure throughout your life; that you can replace those patterns with productive ones, through acknowledging whatever irrational beliefs or angry thinking motivate them; and most importantly, that no-one but *you* can do this for you. I hope also to demonstrate that it is possible to receive advice and sometimes even *practical* assistance from spiritual beings in the non-physical dimensions, by requesting it ... not in any humble or religious way, but in an upright, person-to-person way.

Once you recognise these facts, you will open the way for the highest aspects of your nature to evolve and to express themselves, resulting in refreshing transformations in your life. Seeing this, others will be inspired to follow your example, resulting in the gradual spread of accord in society and hopefully, eventually the world.

In Chapters 1-10, therefore, through a step-by-step process, I invite you to look at any possible misconceptions you hold about yourself and others, the choices you make that determine what your future experiences are likely to be, your *reasons* for making those choices and any underlying emotions that drive you to do so.

I also invite you to see why you have the nature you have, how that nature is contributing to your life right now, how you might improve or even change the course of your life through changing certain aspects of your nature and that all that is necessary to achieve this, is a simple *change of mind*.

In Chapters 11-14, I then invite you to consider concepts that Freda Dodd introduced to me and that have had such a profound influence on my life. Because I feel it to be so important to recognise the likelihood that there is a purpose to life, I discuss briefly the other aspect of human existence: that of the non-physical dimensions, to which I believe we all eventually return.

This is not to say that we should constantly focus on the non-physical dimension, but rather, that we should simply cast an occasional eye to it. We are, after all, currently living in a material dimension and that should therefore be our focus. However, occasionally varying our focuses will enable us to maintain a sense of what we can usefully be doing while we are here and of our relationship with the vastness that lies beyond.

Consequences of our intentions and conduct

With the foregoing in mind, I do not personally see how it can be feasible for our conduct and intentions to be irrelevant to us after we die, or for any indebtedness we incur, *never* to be discharged. If I am correct, our conduct and intentions must logically contribute to two aspects of our ongoing existence. The first would be the quality of that existence in any *non-physical* dimension in which we eventually find ourselves (wherever that may be). The second would be the quality of our existence in any *physical* dimension to which we may later be 're-born'.

For this reason I discuss how life might continue for us after we 'die' and the likelihood of returning to this (or some other) physical dimension, to continue our learning processes where we left off. I also discuss the principle of mental communication, in which we undoubtedly engage subconsciously and by which we can receive subtle inspirations from higher spiritual sources, if we choose.

Open your mind

Please don't feel the need either to accept or reject what you read in these pages. Whatever your views, or the strength of your beliefs, my suggestion is that you maintain an open mind to what you read. We all tend to dismiss ideas that contradict our long-held beliefs, or 'logical' perspectives, as were those of manned flight, electricity and radio-waves, not a hundred years ago. In being open to such ideas, however, you can see if there can be any value in them for you and, if so, benefit from the information.

So when encountering an idea that you consider improbable, rather than think, *'That cannot possibly be true!'*, it may be more productive to ask yourself, *'Can it possibly be true?'* Even though an idea may seem improbable, or inapplicable to you, there may be some value in being open to it. Being open does not mean accepting it as 'true'. It simply means accepting it as a 'possibility'. This allows you to explore the unusual, leading to invaluable solutions in your life that you would not otherwise find, or changes that you would not otherwise make.

For instance, on page 54 there are suggestions as to why people hunt. Even if you abhor hunting and you are sure none of the propositions applies to you, there may be some value in looking at them as if you enjoyed the occupation. Perhaps you will discover something about a particular aspect of your nature, or character 'trait', that you had overlooked ... one that *had* in fact been impinging on your life without your realising it. You can then change that aspect of your nature if you choose and in this way improve the conditions in your life.

There is of course a natural tendency to resist change. We all feel more secure with the familiar, thinking and doing what we have always thought and done. Yet, I am sure you will agree, if we continue to do in life only what we have always done, we should expect out of life only what we have always had.

Reconsider your beliefs

The extent to which you are willing to be open to new ideas is determined by the extent to which you are willing to question beliefs that you have always assumed to be true. As we see in Chapter 5, those beliefs determine the decisions you make each day. Mostly originating in your early years, they are influencing what you think, say and do in relation to yourself, the people around you and, ultimately, the broader sphere of those with whom you interact in your life. They are also influencing how they are in turn behaving toward you.

As a result of this chain reaction, your beliefs (and misconceptions) as to what is right, wrong, good, bad, godly, sinful, intelligent, unrealistic, too idealistic and so on, are determining the directions you are taking currently and your long-term destiny.

Some beliefs, such as *'there is a higher being watching everything we do'*, can be productive and lead to the evolution of the higher aspects of our nature and well-being. Others, such as *'every man for himself'*, can cause not only those higher aspects to be suppressed, but lower ones to be reinforced, resulting in antisocial and possibly even barbaric behaviour. This can attract people with similar tendencies into our lives and, in turn, situations that cannot be reversed.

The moment you change your mind as to some of the beliefs you hold, any counter-productive patterns of behaviour related to those beliefs will spontaneously begin to evaporate. This will in turn change the people and situations you attract to yourself and the re-direction your life then takes.

Changing your mind in this way will not always be easy. It will sometimes demand determination, patience and even courage, particularly where it is inconvenient to do so, or where it involves having to acknowledge what is true or untrue about the world, religion and yourself, contrary to what you have always believed, or prefer to believe. But, as you will quickly discover, the rewards through making those changes will far outweigh the inconvenience of doing so.

Now, prepare to embark upon a journey of introspection and change ... a journey that, if you allow it, will open the way for the evolution of your highest nature and for more success, friendships and love to come into your life.

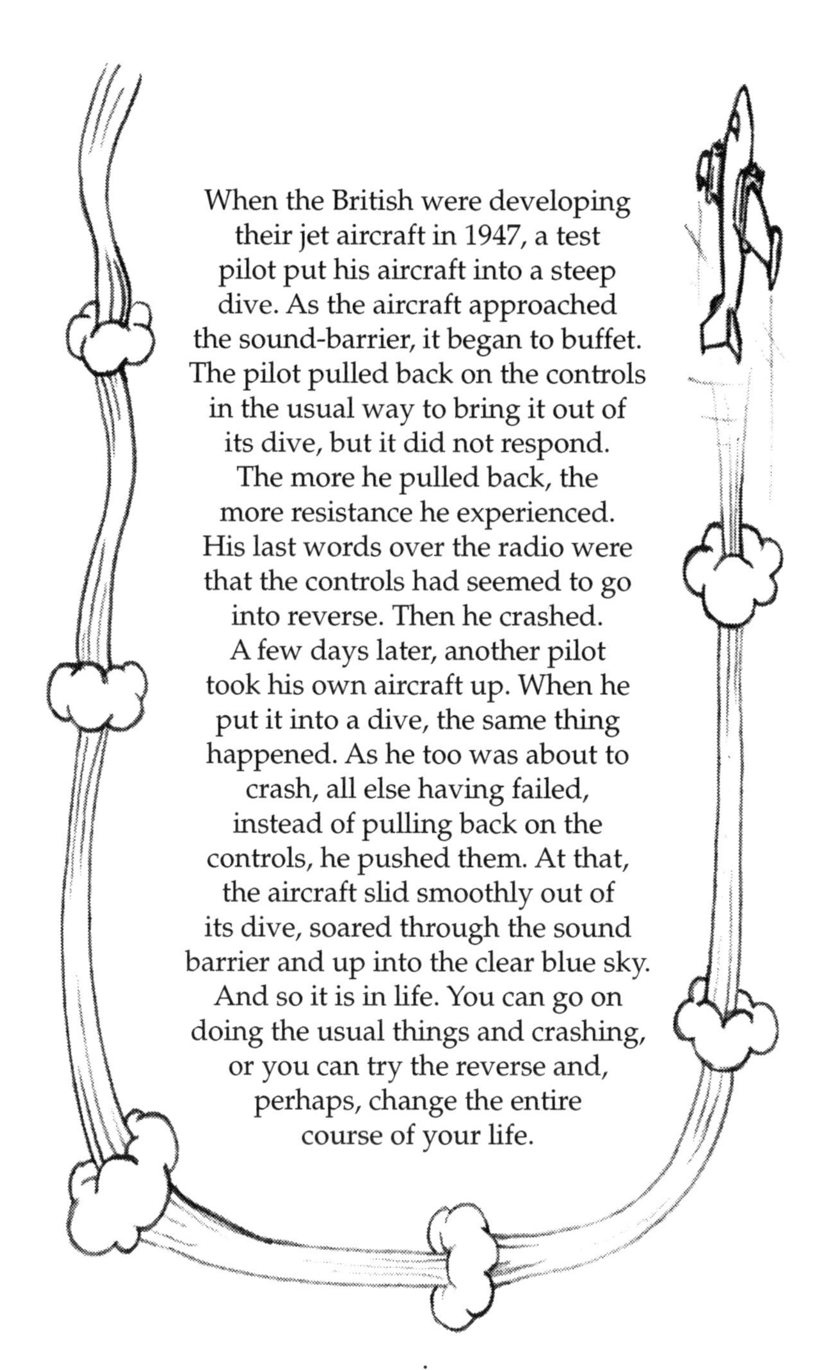

When the British were developing their jet aircraft in 1947, a test pilot put his aircraft into a steep dive. As the aircraft approached the sound-barrier, it began to buffet. The pilot pulled back on the controls in the usual way to bring it out of its dive, but it did not respond. The more he pulled back, the more resistance he experienced. His last words over the radio were that the controls had seemed to go into reverse. Then he crashed. A few days later, another pilot took his own aircraft up. When he put it into a dive, the same thing happened. As he too was about to crash, all else having failed, instead of pulling back on the controls, he pushed them. At that, the aircraft slid smoothly out of its dive, soared through the sound barrier and up into the clear blue sky. And so it is in life. You can go on doing the usual things and crashing, or you can try the reverse and, perhaps, change the entire course of your life.

CHAPTER ONE

Your Journey Called 'Life'

Have you ever watched a fly trying to get out of the window? For hour after hour the fly will try to penetrate the glass. Because it is so close to the problem, however, it does not see why it cannot do so. Whatever you might do to help the fly, by opening the window and perhaps guiding it with your hand, it disregards that help. Instead, it repeatedly batters itself against the glass, never pausing to consider the alternative being offered. Unless it eventually finds its way out by chance, it passes its entire lifetime never knowing that there was that alternative.

Life is a journey of learning and of change. It is as if we are travelling on an endless upward escalator, along which we have three options to:

- make some effort to progress,
- make no effort and simply drift,
- resist the direction in which we are being carried.

Which of these options have you chosen?

As children, we can all tend to be thoughtless, sometimes even cruel, without understanding the significance of what we are doing. As we mature, we can nurture those tendencies throughout adulthood, or we can replace them with higher aspects of nature that we possess.

What kind of nature do you have?

Does your good nature see you through life, or do you prefer to rely on money, cunning, sexual allure or perhaps physical strength to see you through? Do you have a positive kind of nature, or is it constantly negative? Are you comfortable to be with, or difficult? Aggressive or gentle? Rigid or pliable? Dependable or a risk?

Do you congratulate others for their achievements, or do you resent them? Do you see others as evolving alongside you on their journeys of life, or do you see them as 'opportunities' through which to advance your own interests wherever you can? Do you try to pay your debts on time, or do you delay doing so as long as you can?

Do people readily help you when you are in need, or do they do so grudgingly? Do you *welcome* their help, or do you believe you must 'prove' you can go it alone?

Are you a sanctuary that people seek out, or a minefield, with tripwires that unsuspecting people trigger off at the slightest comment?

Are you quick to forgive, or do you bear grudges for years? Are you spontaneously warm toward others, or do you reserve your warmth for those who are first warm to you?

Is there joy in your voice when you speak, or is there constant irritation? Do you smile a lot, or do you not? Is your smile genuine, or is it a front for what you *really* feel? Are you at peace, or is there a constant battle going on within you and, wherever you, go a potential battleground?

Do you rarely disagree with others, or do you have disagreements every day? In your disagreements, do you acknowledge others' points of view, or brush them aside? Do you apologise when you're wrong, or maintain your 'rightness' to the end?

If you drive and you damage someone's vehicle, do you hurry to take responsibility, or try to evade it? Do you allow others to come into your lane of traffic, or indignantly demand that they wait?

What of your qualities? Is what appears on your surface all there is, or is there more to you than others — and perhaps even you — realise? Do you constantly criticise yourself for your 'weaknesses', or do you congratulate yourself for your 'strengths'? Do you acknowledge your achievements for what they are, or do you measure their worth according to those of others?

If you are a parent, would you want a parent like yourself? Would you want a son or daughter like yourself? If you are searching for someone to share your life, or even if you already have someone, are you the sort of partner he or she would want? More to the point, are you the sort of partner *you* would want?

Choosing to learn through your mistakes

Life is not about not making mistakes; it is about *learning* through our mistakes. Nor is it about what we *do*, but learning *through* what we do. Do you learn through your experiences in life, or are you still making the same mistakes today that you were making years ago?

Our life-experiences provide us with information through which we can learn and evolve, if we choose. Regrettably, we seldom learn through the mistakes of others. We must, it seems, make our own. Otherwise we would all benefit from the wealth of information possessed by the elderly, whose wisdom we seldom respect. So, from the moment of birth until that final breath, life involves having to learn and, often by trial and error, even *unlearn* what we had previously learned.

In terms of personal evolution, all six billion of us on this planet cannot be at an identical point of development. Each of us has his or her particular learning experiences to assimilate. There can be millions of such learning experiences through each lifetime. Some will be simple and easily assimilated. Others will be more complex, repeatedly presenting themselves until their significance is eventually grasped. Some will take just a few moments. Others can take entire lifetimes ... and even longer. The key is to *choose to learn* from these experiences.

29,000 days on planet Earth

On average, in the West, the human lifespan is about 29,000 days. During our time here, we can choose simply to 'exist', letting one day pass after another, controlled by our predicaments and learning nothing from our mistakes. Alternatively, by recognising how we are responsible for at least some of the predicaments we experience, we can adjust our future behaviour accordingly. Then, instead of being controlled by those potential predicaments, looming on the horizon, we can change them.

We all tend to look back on our lives with some sense of regret, often locked into memories from the past. But if, rather than cling to the past, we embrace the changing phases in our lives with dignity through our advancing years, we can not only enjoy our time ahead, but make use of it productively. Any pleasure we have given in certain ways in former years, we can give in other ways, to people and animals, in later years; any wisdom we have acquired, we can utilise to counsel others; and any power we have gained, we can utilise for the benefit of the planet.

Our power

"WE LOST ..."

Our worth is determined not according to the power we *possess*, but according to how we *use* that power. Most people would agree that life should be enjoyed, so long as it is not to the detriment of others. However, in our scramble for fulfilment and in the misconception that this is the only lifetime we will ever know, many of us pursue that fulfilment at the expense of others.

In the commercial world, some of us believe that success has to mean the loss or misfortune of others, unconcerned that their needs may be no less than their own. Some erode the ozone layer, deplete forests and oceans and render species in them extinct. Some ensnare the young, unconcerned that they are the treasured daughters and

"WE WON!"

sons of others. Some violate creatures for amusement, food or experiment, without concern for the suffering they endure. Some practise religious rituals, in the belief that these will yield them exceptional benefits, or privileged places in the 'hereafter', denied to others. Some assume 'divine' authority to themselves, interpret ancient 'scriptures' as they see fit and inculcate into the minds of the impressionable, what they do not know to be true, or what science has shown is not.

Ripples of consequence

Like ripples, created by pebbles thrown into a pond, everything we do affects everyone else over whom those ripples flow. And as, eventually, the ripples reach the furthest banks of our world, they must flow back, if not to us, then to those we leave behind, or to their descendants.

Just as we are experiencing the consequences of pebbles of people from past, others will experience the consequences of our own, far into the future. As history repeatedly attests, one pebble thrown by one enlightened person can contribute to the raising of consciousness in

millions, while another, thrown by just one angry or resentful person, can contribute to indescribable misery.

Within us all are lower, self-serving aspects of nature that originated in our reptilian ancestors of millions of years ago. Some are active in us now. Others are dormant, like microbes, awaiting the right conditions in which to germinate. It is through those same lower aspects of nature that we are all contaminating one another, somehow or other, to create the myriad conflicts on our planet; no less than when we shake hands, exchange money or sneeze openly in confined places.

Love

In contrast to the lower aspects of our nature, are the higher ones, manifesting through what we term 'love'. At its highest, this love manifests in our consideration for others — people and creatures — however insignificant they may seem; in our helping those in need, not out of any sense of duty, or hope for reward, but out of the 'heart felt' desire to do so. It manifests in our identification with others, even those with whom we are in conflict, seeing their hopes, fears and needs as no different to our own and wishing for them the welfare we wish for ourselves. It manifests in our courtesies toward those we do not know; in the pleasure we take in their fulfilment, even where we would have wished that fulfilment for ourselves; in our concern for our customers' needs, placing their interests above our own; and in our consolation at knowing that the taxis we miss in the pouring rain, the parking spots, theatre seats, bargains, prizes and even the love partners we fail to win, are enjoyed by others instead.

Everyone would prefer to manifest the highest levels of love that reside in their nature. It is only the intrusion of suspicion, fear, anger and misconception that obstruct this manifestation. Yet if we all took responsibility for replacing the lower aspects of our nature with the higher ones we possess, that obstruction would gradually diminish. Instead of discord, there would then be greater respect and cooperation; and those who are in conflict with one another would admire the excellence of one another's higher nature instead. That higher nature, inherent in every one of us and in every culture of our planet, would then emerge and be shared, toward an increasingly enlightened and flourishing world.

The past is past...

... nor you are what you were even one moment ago. Through constantly being mindful of this fact, you can accelerate the changes in your nature and advance more rapidly from your present levels of consciousness and existence, to higher ones. By scrutinising the patterns of your behaviour, replacing those that are counter-productive to you and to those around you, you can improve what occurs not only in your own life, but in the lives of those among whom you live and work.

Through the slightest shift in your *intentions*, you can create this change. As this occurs, you will find yourself attracting similarly minded people and advancing more rapidly toward a more productive, purposeful and enjoyable life. And the more conscious you are of this fact, the more life's opportunities will open up to you in surprising ways. As always, of course, the *choice* is yours.

. . .

This book is filled with metaphors. One metaphor I like is of each of us being a unique diamond, through which the light that shines varies in colour and brilliance, according to our facets and their clarity.

Whatever your age or circumstances, you have the opportunity to work at clearing any imperfections and polishing and adding new facets to your nature. Whether you live a full and chaotic life, or you are at the point of looking back in quiet contemplation, I hope this book proves to be of value to you and that the light that shines through you becomes ever more brilliant, beautiful and an inspiration to others.

Prepare for change.

CHAPTER TWO

Your Nature

Whatever the life forms on this planet, they possess brains to organise them according to their environments. Those life forms range from the elementary crustaceans of the ocean, with brains consisting of just one neuron (our original ancestors, according to Darwin) to the human, with brains of such complexity as to be beyond our comprehension.

Actually, what we refer to as the 'human brain' comprises seven or more brains, each of which developed during a different period over the 380 million years of our evolution. Even so, each of those brains continues to run our systems and influence us today, just as it did in those times.

During the final 80 million years of our evolution, our two newest brains (the neo-cortex) evolved to provide us with the means to control our bodies as we choose and to talk. To varying degrees, those same brains also occur in many creatures; apes, dogs, cats, rats, pigs, horses, elephants, seals, dolphins, whales and some birds to name a few. Those of us who enjoy close relationships with our pets will know how they 'talk' to us in their respective ways.

Our two new brains also enable us to perform intellectual tasks. As a result of the 'thought-images' that appear in our minds, we calculate, conceptualise, invent, reason, empathise, hold beliefs and anticipate the future. So sophisticated have these two brains become that they also enable us to modify previously established patterns of behaviour, even in our older brains, however deep rooted some of these patterns may be.

Neurons and pathways (in a nutshell)

The brain is composed of hundreds of billions of electrical circuits, or 'neural pathways', along which electrical charges carry instructions throughout the body. These pathways are formed by the neurons themselves, which grow extensions that link together in response to demands for new tasks to be performed.

The more efficient particular behaviour proved to be for the creatures of millions of years ago, the more active the pathways that prompted that behaviour became; and, like muscles, the stronger they became. Eventually, this resulted in automatic or 'instinctive' patterns of behaviour, the combination of which is what we refer to as our 'nature'.

Learning to play a musical instrument is a representation of this process. Initially, the process of learning to play causes new pathways to be created; the more a person plays, the more reinforced those pathways become. Eventually, patterns develop, resulting in the ability to do so automatically. If that person's child learns to play in due course, the pathways he or she has inherited become further reinforced and so on.

Patterns from millions of years ago

Today, when we are in similar situations to those of our ancestors, even our reptilian ancestors of 100 million years ago, charges travel along the same pathways in our brains, which then prompt — or *drive* — the same patterns of behaviour in us, as they did our ancestors. Hence, those

sometimes overwhelming drives with which we are all familiar.

Some pathways prompt selfish, antisocial and animalistic patterns of behaviour, vestiges of which can be latent in any one of us. Then we lie, cheat, steal, betray, lie in wait, fight over territories and females, hunt, assault, invade, kill, hold to ransom, ignore the plight of the helpless, or leave others to pay for offences we ourselves have committed.

In contrast, when permitted to do so, other pathways prompt the higher aspects of our nature, instead. Then we share, support, nurture, cooperate, behave nobly, show compassion and love. Examples of many of these patterns can readily be observed among our primate cousins in the jungle ... or in many a school playground.

In addition to patterns that are active in us now, are others that are dormant, but nevertheless available, to spring into action when needs or situations demand. Some of those patterns will be superficial. Others will be at the very cores of our nature, prompting us in their respective ways throughout our lives until we eliminate them.

In the neurons of your new brains today, through the accumulated experience of hundreds of ancestors over thousands of years, you possess abilities, talents and *greatness* of which you may be totally unaware, waiting to be awakened.

Switches and intentions

As to which patterns of behaviour are active in us and which are not is determined by switches, or 'synapses', located at the hundreds of billions of points at which our neurons have linked together, throughout the resulting networks of our neural pathways. Through an electrochemical process, these switches turn on and off, allowing charges to pass, or preventing them from doing so, thereby enabling or preventing particular behaviour to occur. The question then is, 'What determines the positions of those switches?'

In primitive creatures, two factors are their previous experience and any information they have inherited as to their ancestors' experience. In us, however, there is an additional factor. That factor is 'intention'.

When we intend anything, images of what we intend appear in our minds, causing switches to go on and off, resulting in our being prompted to put those images into action, or otherwise. As to what we *intend* is determined by whether we believe the outcome will be pleasurable, painful, productive, counter-productive, right, wrong and so on.

Promptings from your pathways

Everything you think, say and do, every emotion you experience and every decision you make is the result of activities along your pathways, according to the configurations of the switches throughout your seven brains. At this very moment, billions of switches are going on and off inside your head, connecting and disconnecting pathways, prompting you to behave in particular ways and not to behave in others.

Although *prompted* by your pathways, what you feel,

think, say and do is either an instinctive response, or one you have chosen. As with your muscles, however, you have the power to choose how you will respond to these promptings in various situations. Sometimes you will respond instinctively and at other times out of choice; sometimes through your 'outraged' pathways and at other times, your 'sweet-as-honey' pathways; sometimes your 'business-is-business' pathways and other times, your 'noble' pathways; sometimes through your heart and other times your intellect; and so on.

Your intentions are the solution

So long as any charge is permitted to flow along a particular pathway, that pathway will continue to prompt the same behaviour. The less it is permitted to do so — in other words, the more it is *forbidden* to prompt particular behaviour — the less potential it will have in the future. Merely to refrain from behaving in a certain way occasionally, or grudgingly, does not reduce a pathway's potential. This still leaves it available to prompt the same behaviour again, when similar situations arise.

The only way not to be prompted by a particular pathway and to be prompted by another in its place is consistently to *intend* this. Then the switches connecting it will increasingly remain off, changing your nature that little bit. This has an important domino effect, because that one modification causes a whole array of other switches to reconfigure themselves, changing your nature that little bit more.

The reason for this is that each pathway is linked to thousands of others, prompting them all with its particular behaviour. For instance, a 'loving' pathway may be connected to a 'parental' pathway, a 'partnership' pathway, an 'employer' pathway, an 'employee' pathway and so on, prompting loving behaviour in each role. Likewise, an 'aggressive' pathway, a 'judgemental' pathway, a 'betrayal' pathway and so on, each prompting that behaviour throughout every aspect of one's life.

So, for instance, if a pathway, responsible for 'betrayal' in certain areas of one's life, is disconnected and replaced by one that prompts honourable behaviour, all the other pathways that were originally connected to it will become influenced by the 'honourable' one instead.

Consider the relaxing pastime of angling: Leaving aside the question of whether or not fish feel pain, or whether it is reasonable to fish in order to eat, or even whether they are released after being caught, when we fish with hooks, we intend to deceive the creatures into believing the bait we are offering is something they will enjoy. In other words, when we fish in this way, we intend to 'betray'.

However inconsequential this may *seem*, the point is that while we are in the process of betraying the fish, we are causing charges to flow along our 'betrayal' pathways. In so doing, we reinforce them and thus reinforce the instinctive mechanism to betray ... not just when fishing, but in every other major and seemingly inconsequential aspect of our lives. This process applies to every pattern of our behaviour, ranging from that of the primitive 'hunting' instinct to the most evolved of 'empathising' with others.

Differing configurations, differing natures

Essentially, we all have the same pathways in our brains. What differentiates the nature of each of us is how those

pathways are wired up … in other words, how the switches along them are configured. The question, then, is how we come to have those differing configurations in the first place.

One factor, *not to be ruled out*, is the nature we already possessed prior to being born, which we brought with us in our unconscious memories when we took occupation of our embryos. Another factor is our parents' configurations, according to the natures they possessed, which we inherited at our moments of conception. No less than in animals, these included any they had inherited from their parents, which they had not modified up to that time and so on, all the way back along the long lines of our ancestors, to the earliest creatures from which we descend.

Your dormant nature

Since we have inherited some of our ancestors' configurations, it follows that we have also inherited some aspects of their nature. This does not mean we will necessarily *behave* as they did. Inherited configurations simply provide us with *propensities* to behave in certain ways, some of which will be active in us and others dormant.

Even so, these dormant propensities can be triggered off in us at any time according to our situations, such as when we feel threatened, when we feel betrayed, when we are under the influence of alcohol or drugs, when our desires outweigh our senses of duty, when we have power and when we love. Even if they are never triggered off in us, we can still be the carriers of those propensities, transmitting them genetically to our descendants. If you have children or grandchildren, you may see tell-tale signs of those you possess, through subtle patterns that you recognise in them.

Evidence of these propensities in ourselves can be identified through the films and literature we enjoy and the characters with which we identify. However compassionate, loveable, eminent, religious or spiritual we may be, we can still feel aroused by those depicting warfare, violence or animalistic behaviour, as charges are triggered into flowing along pathways that provide for such behaviour.

At the same time, of course, however much we may spend life in warring, violent or animalistic ways, we can still be inspired by films and literature that depict loving, compassionate, spiritual and noble behaviour. And as we know, many nations, notorious for their barbarism in distant times, are renowned for propagating the highest standards of morality on this planet today!

As you can see, all this has important implications. Since our natures change as our intentions change, in changing our intentions, we change not only our own lives, but through the nature we disseminate to our offspring, also the lives of the thousands of generations that are to descend from us, far into the unforeseeable future.

Father and Son

A man was bathing with his son in a spa, high in the snowy mountains of ancient Persia. 'My son,' said the father, 'I am thirsty. Fetch me some water, that I may drink.' Taking up a jug, the son dutifully ran barefoot to a nearby stream and, filling it with clear fresh water, returned to his father, saying, 'Here, father, drink.'

Years later the son became a father, to bathe with *his* son in the same spa. 'My son,' he said, 'I am thirsty. Fetch me some water, that I may drink.' Taking up a jug, the son scooped some melting slush from the edge of the spa and turning to his father, said, 'Here, father, drink.'

Pondering a moment, the father said, 'When I was a boy many years ago, bathing with my father in this spa, he bade me fetch him some drinking water. At once I ran barefoot to that stream and hurried back to him with clear fresh water. If this is *my* reward, what will *yours* be?'

Your Memory System

You will be familiar with the way a tune or scent can take you back many years, arousing emotions deep within you. So much so, you can recall situations, places and even the weather, just by hearing a tune or smelling a scent once again. Memorabilia are examples of how we can be taken back to poignant memories, especially those of childhood.

Incorporated throughout the neurons of the brain is a memory system, which records every item of information that has ever reached it through the senses. These records also include emotions associated with those experiences, even from as far back as in the womb (and, perhaps, even before).

When information reaches the brain, whether through the senses or the thought process, it causes any similar or related information to be retrieved from the memory and to appear in the mind. That information may be in the form of a word, scent, taste, colour, shape, texture, sound, accent, tone of voice, situation and so on. The effect of this is that new information is compared with that already on record, enabling the most advantageous decisions to be reached toward survival, or betterment.

The typical consequence of this process is that we tend to feel attracted to people with the same names, appearance or behaviour as those we have liked in the past and disinclined toward any we have disliked. On a more subtle level, we can even feel attracted to or repelled by people according to common *intentions* that we exchange subliminally; higher intentions attracting those of higher consciousness and primitive intentions, those of primitive consciousness. So if you complain of constantly attracting to yourself the same kind of person or situation, it may be that you are subconsciously seeking that kind of experience.

For instance, if someone associates an intense, early romantic or intimate encounter with an experience of fear, pain, rejection or betrayal, in some convoluted way, there could be an inclination to seek relationships that re-created such an experience. If the association were of security and of being loved, on the other hand, the inclination would be to seek partners who provided these. In this way, the experiences of childhood and adolescence form the foundations for our later needs and behaviour in adulthood.

Emotional associations from the past

In itself, 'information' is neutral and does not produce any emotion. However, if one's *attitude* toward certain information is not neutral, charges are generated whenever that information 'comes to mind', producing the emotion of love, compassion, fear, jealousy, anger, resentment, sadness, sense of guilt and so on.

Just as pleasurable incidents in life cause memories of similar experiences from the past to be brought to mind, resulting in a joyful disposition, balanced emotions, peaceful mind and spontaneous self-expression, each irritating incident brings forward memories of other such experiences. Until the pain associated with these experiences is 'neutralised', the result is the tendency toward an angry disposition, inner rage and rash or antagonistic behaviour, without the explanation being recognised. Evidence of such emotionally 'charged' memories reveals itself in our tones of voice and handwriting, through which our emotions find expression.

There is a device known as an electro-galvanometer, which can detect through the hands when charged memories are passing through the mind. Through this device, traumas can be traced back to earliest years (and, it is thought, even to previous lifetimes). However, as we shall see in Chapter 10, through 'releasing' the causes of these traumas, their effects can become neutralised and the mind liberated from them.

Your mind and consciousness

You might envisage your mind as a multi-dimensional, holographic screen, where images appear as the result of electrical charges travelling along the pathways in the brain (for which reason the mind seems to be in the head). When we observe those images, we describe ourselves as being 'conscious'. For our purposes, consciousness may simply be regarded as 'awareness'; the more aware we are of these images, the more 'expanded' our conscious may be said to be. So, as a new born infant, you were simply conscious of the textures, voice and scent of your mother. As you grew older, your senses developed and your consciousness of her expanded. Then, perhaps, you became conscious of your father, other infants, your environment and later, your responsibilities to the society in which you live and the world.

When observing an aeroplane in the sky, you may simply be conscious of it as 'an aeroplane', or have a more expanded consciousness of it as a machine that flies, in which are people, reading, talking, eating and sleeping.

When passing people in the street, or working with them, you may simply be conscious of them as 'other people', or have a more expanded consciousness of them as 'other beings' on their respective paths of development, each with similar hopes, needs and problems as yourself.

When selling something, you may simply be conscious of the benefit you are gaining, or have a more expanded consciousness of the contribution the buyer is making to your life and the contribution you are making to his or hers.

When observing an animal or other creature, even the minutest of insects, you may simply be conscious of it as 'just a creature', or have a more expanded consciousness of it as another form of consciousness, with comparable needs, sense of trust and betrayal and intensities of joy, anguish, pleasure and pain to your own.

When looking up at the night sky, you may simply be conscious of billions of 'stars', or have a more expanded consciousness of them as planets, some of which may be worlds like your own, inhabited by other beings, like or unlike yourself.

Your consciousness need not be confined to observing the physical dimension alone. It may expand to other dimensions and, through the application of your 'sixth sense', or 'intuition', reveal what would not be accessible to you simply through the intellectual or logical approach.

Ultimately, what you permit yourself to be conscious of — or rather, what you do not *prevent* yourself from being conscious of — determines the levels and dimensions of your consciousness. The more you permit, the more conscious you become. The more you prevent, the more limited your consciousness remains.

You might imagine the night sky as an analogy of your consciousness: the brighter the sky, the more images you are permitting to appear in your mind and so the more expanded is your consciousness. Conversely, the more you are suppressing, the more they are being obscured, to leave only a few pin-pricks of light dotted about. How bright or dark is the night sky of your consciousness?

SUMMARY

- ♣ Your nature is the sum total of your potential patterns of behaviour.
- ♣ Those patterns are determined by the switching configurations throughout your neural pathways.
- ♣ Until the positions of the switches have been modified, permanently, your pathways continue to provide you with the same propensities as your ancestors and any primitive creatures to which you are related.
- ♣ Propensities can remain dormant in you without being active and, where you do not eliminate them, passed on to your descendants.

Gain a sense of how you can modify the switching arrangements along your neural pathways

1 Think of someone whom you dislike in some way:
   a) Begin judging or criticising that person in your mind.
   b) Now change your mind and, instead, see something admirable in him or her.
   c) How do you feel about that?

2 Think of a situation that has disappointed, annoyed or upset you.
   a) Decide to change the pathway that prompts that feeling and engage a different one.
   b) How do you feel now?

3. Think of a pathway in your brain that you engage a lot in your day-to-day life, which prompts:
   a) a productive pattern that you would like to reinforce.
   b) an unproductive pattern that you would like to change.

Constantly review your pathways and expand your consciousness.

CHAPTER THREE

Changing Your Patterns

The Man Who Thought He Was a Mouse

For several years a man consulted a therapist, thinking he was a mouse. One day sometime later, he saw a cat. Turning on his heels he ran to the therapist's house and banging on the door, pleading to be let in. 'What seems to be the matter?' the therapist asked. 'A cat ...' the man cried. '... I've just seen a cat!' 'My dear fellow,' the therapist assured him, 'we have established you're not a mouse.' 'Yes, doctor,' the man replied, '*I* know that and *you* know that. But does the *cat*?'

However great our achievements in life, if during our formative years we ever felt 'bad', 'stupid', 'useless', 'incompetent', 'undeserving' or 'unwanted', unless the charge on them has since been neutralised, memories of those feelings can continue to lurk at the 'backs of our minds', not only driving us incessantly to 'prove' ourselves in various ways throughout our lives, but also causing us to suppress the beauty, wisdom, excellence and greatness of our nature.

In the process, believing the descriptions to be true of us and overlooking the fact that we possess those higher aspects of nature, we may fall into the trap of seeing only lower aspects in ourselves and cultivate patterns of behaviour that express these alone.

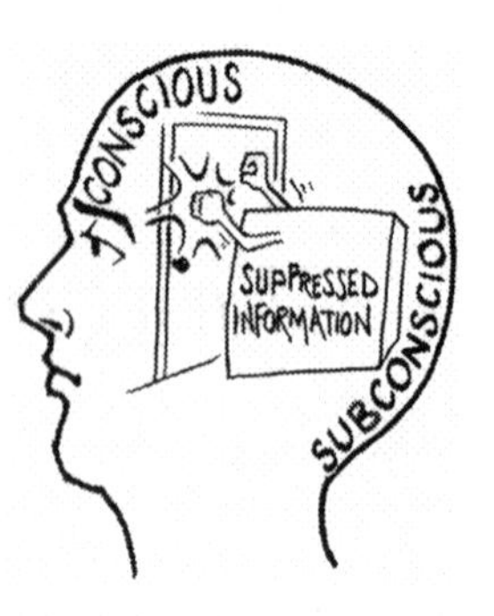

Even so, the higher aspects will persistently pound on the doors of our consciousness, *demanding* to be acknowledged. The result: stress, inner rage and confusion.

Eradicating your unwanted patterns

Since, for every pattern of behaviour, there is a pathway that prompts it, if you want to eradicate a particular pattern, you must reduce the charge travelling along the pathways that prompt it. There are two ways to do this. One is through the natural process of evolution by which primitive creatures, which cannot reason, do so.

The difference between yourself and primitive creatures is that *you* can reason. So if you would prefer to enjoy a happier life now, rather than wait several hundred thousand years before doing so, there is an alternative. That alternative is *consciously* to disengage your lower pathways and engage your higher ones in their places, so that the higher aspects of your nature are given precedence to express themselves and the lower are effectively eliminated. To be able to do this, however, you must first acknowledge these aspects of your nature ... both lower and higher.

Of course, it's very easy to speak of engaging and disengaging pathways, but, in practice, how can this be achieved? The answer is *little by little, day by day.* If you genuinely intend this, the switches along them *will* change ... and if you do not, they will not.

Free the higher aspects of your nature

For the higher aspects of your nature to be free to express themselves, it is also necessary to acknowledge and rectify any erroneous beliefs that obstruct them. Then, any stress, rage and confusion arising from these are eliminated and those higher aspects spontaneously express themselves.

There is a difference between intending to replace a lower pathway with a higher one through the hope of getting some benefit and doing so through the belief that it is 'right' to do so. When you intend to replace a pathway because you believe it is 'right', there is a simultaneous intention not to re-engage that pathway and your nature begins the process of change. But if your intention is to replace it through the hope of some benefit, the pathway remains intact, available for future opportunities.

Keep this in mind as you work through this book. In so doing you will discover that you do have the ability, if you choose, to change your counter-productive patterns and in so doing, much of what would otherwise occur in your life.

Fear, the obstacle to change

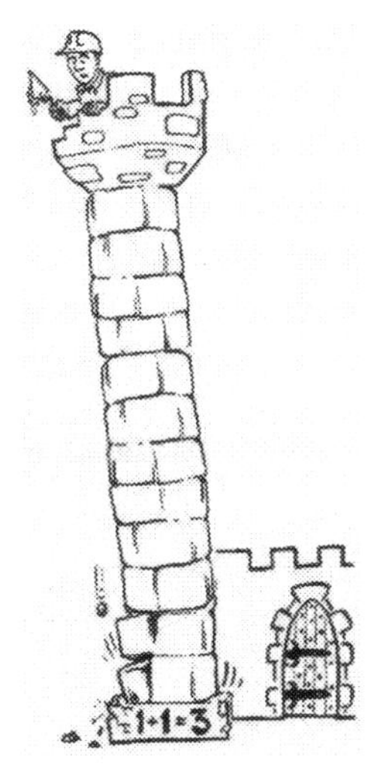

It is important to recognise that if we fear that in acknowledging any lower aspects of our nature, we will be admitting to 'defects' in ourselves, we may be reluctant to do so. Instead, we may be tempted to go through life trying to deceive the world and ourselves into believing they do not exist.

So the question is this: Can it be to our benefit to live lives of self-deception, building castles upon decaying foundations that must eventually collapse? Or is it wiser to acknowledge that what we think, feel, say and do is in response to promptings from our neural pathways, thereby not only enabling ourselves to improve, but enabling our brains to serve us more productively?

Of course, it is only natural to want to deny the existence of lower aspects of nature in ourselves. We all have images of ourselves, or rather, how we would like to see ourselves. Yet, it is only through the willingness to acknowledge the *possibility* that those lower aspects exist, that we can ever really eliminate them.

'Look at me' patterns of behaviour

Because we imagine that if others knew or *believed* particular things about us, they might reject us, we tend to cultivate 'Look at me' patterns, through which, we hope, we will readily be accepted. These patterns can take the forms of roles, masks, attitudes, postures and other ways in which we present ourselves to the world, in the hope of being regarded more favourably and rewarded with respect, acknowledgement, admiration, material benefits, sexual fulfilment and love.

These 'Look at me' patterns begin taking form as we first learn to protect ourselves against disappointment or rejection and so hide our needs or fears. Although the result may be some degree of fulfilment, if we are convinced that we cannot have the experiences we desire *except* through these patterns, we might be tempted to hide, or even *trade off* altogether, some of the higher aspects of our nature in exchange. We might do this to acquire money and power, for instance, believing *these* will bring us our desired experiences.

As the years pass, however, overlooking the original reasons for wanting the money and power, they become our *goals* instead of the means to realise those goals. Then we begin to *identify* with those roles and eventually even come to believe we *are* those roles. In this way we limit, or suppress entirely, the natural inner beauty, excellence and other higher qualities that we possess and that we would otherwise express openly to the world.

Although the reasons for behaving in such ways vary in each of us, they are always prompted by what we *fear losing* if we do not. For example:

Behaviour: I have to be or appear **superior**.
Belief: Otherwise I will not have **approval**.
Fear: Then I will not be **loved**.
Need: Being **loved**
Reasoning: Is more important to me than being **natural.**
Trade off: So I choose to be or appear **superior**.

Here are some other examples of beliefs, fears and needs that can give rise to behaviour that limits the expression of our higher nature. Take a moment to consider these and see which, if any, relate to you:

I have to be or appear —
Rich Strong Intelligent Right Wise Superior Saintly Sceptical Critical Rebellious Stubborn Aggressive Possessive Fashionable Masculine Feminine Desirable Unemotional Unavailable Independent Paternal Maternal Childlike Happy Miserable Angry Helpless Unwell Different.

Otherwise I will not have —
Respect Admiration Acceptance Approval Consideration Control Security Trust Submission

Then I will be —
Vulnerable Powerless Unloved Unimportant Worthless Undervalued Unwanted Rejected Neglected Controlled Excluded Alone

Being —
Secure Strong Powerful Obeyed Admired Accepted Included Loved

Is more important to me than being —
Compassionate Caring Loving Warm Responsible Honest Natural Dignified Sincere Well

So I choose to be or appear etc ...

With this insight into the relationship between the pathways and behaviour, you can, if you choose, set about changing any pattern that limits the expression of your higher nature. Here are two relatively simple steps you may find helpful:

Step 1: Acknowledge your limiting patterns

Think of a 'limiting pattern' in yourself ... one that limits the expression of your excellence, inner beauty, loving, caring or compassionate nature. Then compose a statement that describes that pattern. For example:

My limiting pattern is —

Angry, unforgiving	critic
Superior, rigid	judge
Self-righteous, rejecting	saint
Guilty, undeserving	sinner
Controlling, bossy	tyrant
Resentful, enraged	victim
Aggressive, trouble-seeking	fighter
Helpless, complaining	child
Selfish, inconsiderate	bully
Scheming, deceiving	cheat

Remember, the description you compose is not you. It is a pattern you have cultivated over time to survive, or to gain the love, respect or other rewards you desired.

Once you have acknowledged this pattern, ***stop yourself*** whenever you find yourself expressing it. For example, if you have a tendency to mislead, exaggerate, sit in judgement, be aggressive or find fault with others, stop yourself as you are about to do so.

For the next few days, be aware of the various ways in which you express this behaviour toward those with whom you associate. At the same time, mentally acknowledge your reasons for doing so: *'My reason for doing/saying xxx is ...'*

Step 2: Acknowledge your higher nature

After practising Step 1 for a few days, compose another statement that describes two *higher aspect*s of your nature. These will be the converse of those of your limiting pattern ... ones that most reveal your excellence, inner beauty, sensitivity, loving, caring and compassion. At the same time, *express* those higher aspects wherever you go. For example:

I am –
Peaceable and forgiving.
Neutral and non-judgmental.
Flexible and easygoing.
Compassionate and sympathetic.
Loving and open.
Sensitive and considerate.
Wise and enlightened.

For the next two weeks, constantly remind yourself of this statement as you go through your day, focusing on your intention that your lower pattern be eradicated and your higher pattern cultivated in its place.

Remember that just as you possess primitive pathways in your old brains to help you survive, you have a fine network of higher, more evolved pathways available to you in your two new brains (neo-cortex), which will become active and prompt new patterns in you, *the moment* you begin intending to engage them. Eventually, these new patterns will be as automatic as the previous ones were and your nature will change.

Go for gradual change

Be considerate to yourself. Don't insist on total change all at once. Go for gradual change that you can monitor. If there seem to be no results, don't feel discouraged. Persevere. There *are* results. You just may not be noticing them. If you say or do something you had determined not to say or do, don't criticise yourself. Quietly acknowledge your reason for having done so and intend to succeed a little more in the future. You might also give your brain a directive to stop prompting you in that way, telling it what you prefer instead. For example:

'Don't prompt me constantly to judge/criticise/find fault with people/myself. Prompt me to be understanding, considerate, neutral, etc.'

The equipment in your head is highly sensitive and sophisticated. Treat it with respect. Then, with each change you make, a whole array of other valuable changes will follow spontaneously.

Keep sight of your ultimate goal

It can be tempting constantly to remind yourself of your regrets, judge others and yourself, retaliate when you feel offended and hold onto feelings of anger to justify your behaviour in various ways. It can also be tempting to lower your standards of integrity when dishonest opportunities are readily at hand, particularly when others can be seen exploiting such opportunities.

However, the evolution of your higher nature and consciousness depends upon your resolve to regulate and alter your own behaviour. And the responsibility for this is yours alone.

So, as you go about your day, constantly remind yourself of the higher aspects of your nature, particularly when limiting patterns show signs of undermining your resolve. Above all, whenever you find yourself becoming misaligned from 'the truth', ***stop*** and realign yourself with it. As you do this, your higher patterns will gain prominence, your limiting patterns will fade, your finest qualities and innermost beauty and excellence will express themselves in their place and your life *will* change.

Two wolves

A Native American was sitting with his grandson at the bank of a river, watching the water washing over the rocks. 'I feel as if there are two wolves wrestling within me,' the old man mused to his grandson. 'One is vengeful, angry and violent ... the other is loving, compassionate and peaceable.' 'Which one is going to win?' the boy asked.' The old man became silent, observing the wolves in his mind. 'The one I nurture,' he replied at last.

SUMMARY

- ♣ The experiences of your early years are the foundations for your patterns of behaviour today.
- ♣ To eliminate unwanted patterns, you must reduce the charge that flows along the pathways that prompt them.
- ♣ To achieve this you must acknowledge the existence of those pathways and intend to replace them with opposite ones.

Recognise your limiting patterns

Consider a limiting pattern of behaviour that you have presented to the world in the past.

a) Which belief drove that pattern?
b) Which need drove the belief?
c) Which fear drove the need?
d) Which higher aspect of your nature did you trade-off?

Be aware of patterns that your brain prompts within you that are not of your higher nature and your reasons for permitting them.

CHAPTER FOUR

Your Power to Choose

During the early parts of our lives we have little if any control over our circumstances. From the time we have control, however, whatever the choices we make, whether after calm reflection or at the height of emotion, they are choices we ourselves make. Even where we feel we are compelled to make certain choices — out of love, anger, fear, pleasure or pain — we nevertheless make those choices. And each time we do so, we initiate courses of events that determine not only our immediate future, but, theoretically, the rest of our lives.

It can seem as if we have no choice over what we *feel*, as we may tell ourselves. But is this entirely true? If you feel offended by someone's remark, for instance, is that person offending you, or is it you offending yourself? If a parrot were to make the same remark, would you still feel offended? If so, since birds (probably) don't have opinions, what you feel must be due to an opinion, or fear, you hold about yourself, which is being aroused by that remark.

There is much value to be gained in recognising the extent to which you are responsible for the choices you make — even those made under pressure — and the consequences of those choices, not only to yourself, but also to others. Once you accept the principle, you will find yourself exercising greater control over the circumstances in your life through making more considered choices and so forestalling some consequences that might otherwise occur.

The consequences of your choices

The choices you make in life are determined by what you consider more important than something else at the time, such as money, love, freedom and possessions.

Taking financial risks in the hope of gaining greater comfort, security or status, for instance, may be more important to you than the prospect of any loss this might incur. Safeguarding against rejection by hiding your intentions or wishes, may be more important than the alternative possibility of receiving what you desire. Feeling relaxed through smoking, may be more important than the possibility of contracting lung cancer. Eating more than your body requires, to recall pleasing memories from infancy, or to compensate for some lack of emotional fulfilment, may be more important than having a healthy weight. Maintaining erroneous beliefs, or unproductive patterns of behaviour, may be more important than the inconvenience of adjusting to more plausible beliefs, or more productive patterns.

Not making a choice when some choice needs to be made, leaving 'circumstance' or 'fate' to eliminate the alternatives, may be more important than making a wrong choice, or taking responsibility for your life. Feeling

'right' by maintaining resentments against others for years, may be more important than forgiving them and enjoying harmony, inner peace and improved health. Insisting on your lawful 'rights', may be more important than the possible benefits of conceding, or letting go.

How you create, promote or allow what occurs in your life

Whatever the choices you make, they result in courses of events that you have created, promoted or allowed. Imagine that in a field there is an ill-tempered bull. If you go into the field knowing the bull is there, you *promote* a potential disaster for yourself. If you choose to remain in the field after discovering it there, you *allow* that disaster. However, if you *antagonise* the bull once you are there, obviously, you *create* the disaster.

Most of the circumstances in which you find yourself today are those you instigated and the steps you took to reach those circumstances are steps you chose. Unless some external influence interrupts them, therefore, once you choose certain steps, certain consequences must follow. This is the simple law of cause and effect. Yet you can often alter what is due to occur further ahead, by taking different steps.

You might regard the events in your life as a film being projected onto a screen. Clearly, what is on the screen cannot be altered. Nor is it possible to alter what is rolling off the reel, because that is going to occur. Closing your eyes changes nothing. That would be to ignore what was about to unfold. Ultimately, control can be exercised only by you, the projectionist, who has but two options: one is to continue running the film. The other is to replace it.

It follows, then, that if you do not alter a particular course of events in your life where you can, you are choosing the circumstances that are to follow … which may mean you are deriving some satisfaction from maintaining the circumstances exactly as they are.

Being conscious means making choices, one way or another. The pendulum of choice always swings, either to the left or to the right. It never stops.

SUMMARY

- ♣ From the moment you have the freedom to choose, you create, promote or allow at least some of what occurs in your life.
- ♣ If you do not alter a course of events where you can, you choose that course of events and the circumstances that follow.
- ♣ You are responsible to yourself and others, for the consequences of whatever choices you make.

Recognise your control over your situations

1 Recall a situation that was favourable to you.
   a) How did you create, promote or allow it?
   b) How could you have sabotaged it?

2 Recall a situation that was unfavourable to you.
   a) How did you create, promote or allow it?
   b) How could you have prevented it?

3 Is there a current situation that is, or is likely to be, unfavourable to you?
   a) Are you creating, promoting or allowing it?
   b) If so, how can you prevent it?

4 Is there any aspect of your nature that consistently draws an unfavourable response from others?
   a) If so, which changes can you make to your nature that would change that response?
   b) Are you willing to make those changes?
      If not, why not?

5 Which *higher* aspect of your nature consistently draws favourable responses from others?
   a) Would you be willing always to express that particular aspect of your nature?
      If not, why not?

Constantly be aware of how you may be creating, promoting or allowing what is occurring in your life.

Recognise your control over your situation

Recall a situation [illegible] to [illegible]
a) How did you create [illegible] allow it?
b) How would you have managed it?

[illegible]
a) How did you [illegible]
b) How would you [illegible]

[illegible] that [illegible]
[illegible] to you?
a) Are you [illegible] making or allowing [illegible]
[illegible]

[illegible]

[illegible]

CHAPTER FIVE

Your Beliefs and Truth

Crow on the wall

Looking from my window, one sunny morning, I noticed a crow pecking at a low wall around the perimeter of a roof, across the road. Watching more closely, I saw that what the crow was actually pecking was its shadow, which it had obviously mistaken for another crow.

For several minutes the crow hopped to the left and to the right, pecking obsessively at the shadow. As it did so, the shadow followed; the crow's beak meeting its shadow's beak each time with infuriating accuracy. I was wondering whether, unable to extricate itself from this situation, the crow would eventually collapse from exhaustion, when it suddenly hopped *onto* the wall, presumably to approach the problem from a different perspective. At that, the shadow disappeared. The crow stopped for a moment, cocking its head to one side, as if mystified to find the other crow no longer there. Then it flew off, seemingly without another thought.

So it is with us. We can exhaust ourselves all our lives, unable to extricate ourselves from the obsessive shadows in our minds. Or we can consider those shadows from new perspectives, when we may find that many are without reality … and always were.

Your neurons do not always convey 'the truth'

Have you ever awoken from a dream in a panic, relieved to find it *was* only a dream? Yet, during the dream, did it not seem all too real?

The fact that we believe something, does not make it necessarily true. What we believe are simply conclusions generated by the neurons of our brains, based upon information they have received. If that information is inaccurate, their conclusions will also be inaccurate. Railway lines that appear to meet in the distance are an example of this. It is possible to be hypnotised into believing we have experienced what we have not, or that we are what we are not, or even that we can do what we cannot.

Knowledge is not necessarily the truth

We regard information reaching the neurons in our brains as 'knowledge', or 'the truth' and, once adopted, is very difficult to dislodge thereafter. But what appears to be the truth at one point in time can frequently turn out not to have been so later, when more up-to-date information reaches our brains. So, whatever we say we 'know' to be 'true' today, we can 'know' to have been 'untrue' tomorrow.

In point of fact, we do not truly know anything. All we can mean when we say we 'know' something is that this is the best *we* can do, based upon information available to us at the time.

A hundred years ago, for instance, the atom was 'known' to be incapable of being split. Yet, a few years later it was split. Until recently, light was 'known' to be the fastest form of energy in the universe. Yet, science now accepts that this knowledge is likely to be superseded by that of something faster. In time, this too may be superseded by the knowledge of something faster still, perhaps from a more advanced civilisation in this or some other galaxy, in this or some other universe.

How you form your beliefs

If you think about it, you will see that all the beliefs you hold are beliefs you adopted because you assumed, or accepted, that they were true. Each of those beliefs was based upon an earlier one you had adopted and so on, all the way back down the line of your beliefs to its original foundation. When considering a belief you hold, therefore, the question to ask yourself is whether the original foundation was in fact true.

It is very easy to form any belief you choose. All you need do is generate a sequence of images in your mind, which lead to a conclusion, without questioning the practical feasibility of that conclusion. For example:

- The world is flat.
- The universe evolved in just 144 hours (six days).
- Jonah survived in the stomach of a whale for several days.
- Our enemies are all bad people.

Without any available evidence to the contrary, at one time or another all these beliefs were accepted without question and assumed to be true. Based on information now available, however, we know that the world is not flat, the universe did not evolve in 144 hours, Jonah would certainly have been drowned or digested in the whale's stomach within hours of being swallowed and many of our so-called 'enemies' are in fact very good people.

Even so, some of us will go to endless lengths to convince ourselves and others that something is what it obviously is not, or is not what it obviously is. At the end of the day, however, nothing changes the truth ... not what we say, nor what we hope, nor what we believe.

We can, in fact, believe anything we wish. Based on what we hope or fear, we can become so committed to particular beliefs that we can sabotage our own lives and the lives of others. Our beliefs can drive us to be peaceable or angry, loving or hateful — even toward people we will never know — to praise, offend, respect, resent, reward, punish, defend, kill, pretend to be what we are not and pretend not to be what we are.

If you are to take responsibility for your life, you need to be conscious of what you mean by the words *'I believe'* and recognise the difference between 'belief' and 'knowledge':

- *'I believe'* means: 'There is a series of images running through my mind that lead to a conclusion and I adopt that conclusion as 'true'.
- *'I know'* means: 'No information exists in the entire universe that can change what I believe'.

By examining your beliefs in the light of all information that is available to you, you can decide whether those beliefs are likely to be accurate, or if not, how and why you came to adopt them.

How you adopt your beliefs

There are various ways in which you might adopt your beliefs. One way is through formulating them through logic, based upon your experience (or what you *believe* to be your experience). Another is through trusting others and placing the responsibility for your adopting those beliefs on them … in other words, having 'faith'.

"NOW *THERE'S* A NICE BELIEF..."

Many of us adopt beliefs blindly, in the hope that a higher being will judge us favourably if we do … and in the fear that 'He' will judge us unfavourably if we do not. The difficulty with this is that those from whom we blindly adopt such beliefs will either have formulated them for themselves, using their own forms of logic, or have blindly adopted them in turn from others … and so on, like a hall of mirrors, all the way back to the alleged authors of those beliefs, who may, in fact, have said something completely different.

As a result, hundreds of millions of people across the planet are imposing mental illness, sexual deprivation, suffering, injustice and even death on themselves, other people and animals, simply through the blindly adopted beliefs that they are doing it at the behest of a higher being, who will reward them for it, in due course.

Do you ever *refuse* to believe?

There is a classic test for colour blindness, which involves a page of dots in assorted colours, among which is a letter of the alphabet, predominantly in a particular colour. If someone cannot see that letter, he or she is said to be 'blind' to it. If you were subjected to such a test and the letter were invisible to you, you might refuse to believe it existed. If so, could someone who *could* see it convince you to the contrary?

There is a difference between *not* believing something and *refusing* to believe it. *'I do not believe'* may mean *'I do not have any reliable information to convince me'*. However, *'I refuse to believe'* can only mean, *'I am unwilling to be convinced by any information'*.

Four hundred years ago, despite the evidence clearly visible through Galileo's telescope, 'the Church' refused to believe that the earth revolved around the sun. That evidence contradicted their belief, derived from the Bible, that the sun revolved around the earth. If you had been there at that

"NOW THAT I THINK OF IT, THE SUN DOES REVOLVE AROUND THE EARTH..."

time, would you have commended Galileo, or condemned him? Faced with being burned at the stake, Galileo recanted and was freed. Giordano Bruno, who refused, was not as fortunate.

Not wanting not to know

In life, we can sometimes be unwilling to accept that there are alternatives to the ways we have always thought. There is a natural tendency to hold onto familiar or more convenient beliefs, particularly if we have invested energy, money, self-esteem, or our lifetimes in them. Reluctant to acknowledge that we have been mistaken, or that we must make radical changes to our thinking, we may just decide not to look, thereby *ensuring* we do not know. Consider a proposition that most people would say they know is impossible:

> It is believed that the only way to resist gravity is through the use of gas, hot air or powered propulsion; and that it is otherwise impossible to rise bodily from the ground. However, some people are reputed to be able to rise bodily and move about without any physical support, simply through the direction of their mental energies.

The important point here is not whether such a report is true, but what we do with information that does not fit concepts with which we are familiar, or which we can understand intellectually. If we believe that such a method of resisting gravity cannot in any circumstances be possible, we close the doors on any opportunity to benefit from that information, if it *is* true.

Beliefs are like doorways in the mind, which we can open and close as we choose. The more beliefs — or disbeliefs — we adamantly adopt, about ourselves, other people, life or the universe, the more doorways we close. The more doorways we close, the more avenues leading from them we deny ourselves. The more avenues we deny ourselves, the more limited become our opportunities to expand our consciousness, or simply to improve the conditions in our lives.

Whatever you believe or disbelieve is your choice. For your brain to compute information for you as usefully as possible, however, it is crucial that the beliefs you hold are as accurate as possible. If your beliefs are erroneous, your brain will not only constantly re-cycle them back to you thereafter, but will also contaminate all other related information it receives, to provide you with further erroneous computations.

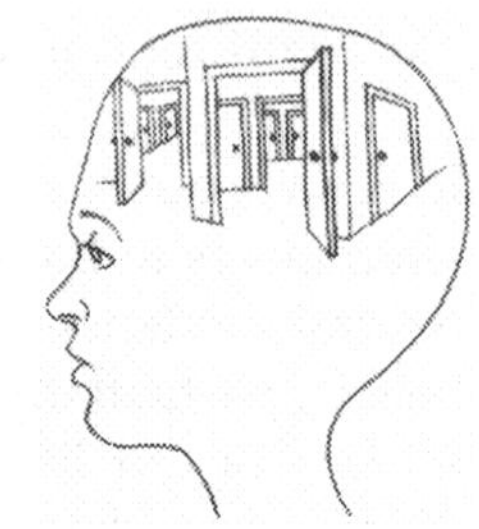

Lanterns in the dark

Even though you may not *know* whether a particular belief is true, there can be much value in holding it, provided you are prepared to update it in the light of fresh information that becomes available. In this way it becomes like a lantern in the dark by which you can explore further. This applies to beliefs on any subject, from the mundane to those of science, extra-sensory phenomena, life after death, religion, God and intelligences on other planets or dimensions.

Adamantly to hold onto any belief that is erroneous, however, must be to choose a course that ultimately leads nowhere. And, until updated, that belief must influence your decisions and behaviour in counter-productive ways throughout your life.

The result can be that you are held back by groundless fears, judgements or feelings of guilt, punishing yourself or

others, or pursuing policies that serve no useful purpose in your life. And, like a rope that tethers a boat to its moorings, that belief must deprive you of the rewards that would otherwise be available to you, preventing you from reaching out to the undiscovered riches that lie beyond the horizons of your mind.

It is essential, therefore, to be ready to adjust any information that has reached your brain, with the most up-to-date 'truths' to which you have access and to examine and modify your beliefs, *or change them altogether*, where they are contradicted by new and more valid information. Only in this way can your brain serve you productively, enabling you to reach more highly evolved levels of consciousness and existence.

SUMMARY

- What you believe is not necessarily the truth.
- Your beliefs are conclusions by neurons in your brain, based on information they receive, which may or may not be accurate.
- You adopt some beliefs either because you want them to be true, or because you fear they may be.
- You are responsible for the beliefs you adopt and for those you cause others to adopt.
- If your brain is to serve you efficiently, the beliefs you hold must be as accurate as possible.

Recognise the difference between your beliefs and the truth

1 Consider a belief you have always held, that you *must* or *must not* do something, or behave in a certain way:
   a) Do you know that belief to be accurate?
   b) If not, are you willing to review it?
      If not, why not?

2 Consider a historical or religious event that you know to be true:
   a) How did you come by this knowledge?
   b) Are you willing to consider that it may not be accurate?
      If not, why not?

3 Consider an unfavourable belief that you hold about someone.
   a) How did you come by this belief?
   b) Are you willing to consider that it may not be accurate?
      If not, why not?

4 Consider an unfavourable belief that you hold about yourself:
   a) How did you come by this belief?
   b) Are you willing to consider that it may not be accurate?
      If not, why not?

Constantly look for 'the truth'.

CHAPTER SIX

Mirrors Everywhere

Just as a camera cannot photograph itself, whatever its lens, we cannot observe ourselves, whatever our intelligence. Instead, we derive perceptions of ourselves through mirrors that are round about us. Whatever we observe — people, animals, plants, inanimate objects, machines, art forms or abstract concepts — they are as mirrors, reflecting aspects of our nature to us, as the neurons of our brains register the similarities between ourselves and them.

Musical instruments are a good analogy: when they are played, any others of the same frequencies nearby vibrate in resonance, 'reflecting' each other's frequencies. You might imagine countless such instruments within yourself, according to the different aspects of your nature, each vibrating in response to those of others.

When we like or dislike what others do, or what they stand for, this touches on aspects of our own nature, which we are either happy to acknowledge or prefer to ignore. So our embarrassment at others' behaviour will not always be due to what they are doing, but rather, to what it triggers off in us. In other words, their behaviour reflects what we believe (or fear) to be true about ourselves ... the greater our *identification* with them, the more intense our responses.

Your identification with others

When we see others displaying emotions, this activates pathways that prompt similar emotions in ourselves. Hence our identification with them. When watching films, we identify with the characters that reflect aspects of our own nature to us. When we watch predators pursuing their prey, as in nature films for instance, we identify with whichever reflect our sense of power or powerlessness. When the prey escapes, we have a sense of disappointment or relief. Likewise, violent or war films, the characters of which enable us to punish others in our minds.

The beauty and excellence that we see in people, children, creatures, plants, nature, music and even inanimate objects, are reflections of aspects of our own nature that we acknowledge as beautiful. Flowers, gardens, music, art, architecture and other works of beauty or excellence that we create, or simply appreciate, are all reflections of the beauty or excellence in our own nature.

Seeing others as 'you'

Subconsciously, what we do to or for others can be what we would wish to be done to or for ourselves in reciprocal situations. Being occupied with cruelty of any kind, whether actively or simply in taking pleasure in the spectacle, can be to identify not only with the tormentors, but also with the victims, experiencing being hunted down, subjugated or tormented for that for which we feel

we deserve to be punished. In the victims' pleas we hear our own.

In contrast, helping even the smaller of insects out of the window or the bath reflects the help we believe we deserve. To save them is to see ourselves being saved. To disregard their plight is to see our own as being disregarded. When giving charity, we are in our minds, vicariously giving to ourselves, because we are identifying with those we are helping. However noble our intentions, our subconscious reasoning will be, 'I know how those people/creatures feel and I would not wish to be in their situations'.

The ways we teach others also tend to be determined by how we feel we should be taught. The more tolerant we are of them, the more tolerant we tend to be of ourselves. The more intolerant we are, on the other hand, or the higher the standards we demand of them, the more intolerant or demanding we may be of ourselves.

When we laugh at others, we are often laughing at ourselves, imagining ourselves in their situations. Hence our favourite jokes. Our criticisms, accusations, cynical suspicions and judgements of others can also frequently reflect feelings we have about ourselves, which we may not wish to acknowledge; and our unquestioning trust in others, the trust we feel can be placed in us.

Children too are mirrors of the children within ourselves. The ways we punish or reward them can reflect the ways we feel we, or the children within us, ought to be punished or rewarded. Depriving them of love is to deprive the children within ourselves of the love we believe we did not deserve when we were children, or do not deserve now. In contrast, the love we lavish on them is the love we want to lavish on the children within ourselves.

In our choices of friends, the more we like our own nature, the more inclined we are to befriend those whose natures reflect our own; and the less we do, the less inclined we will be to do so. Through the principle of the mirror, love partners identify with one another. What they do to or for one another, they are subconsciously doing to or for themselves. So the ways in which we 'reward' or 'punish' one another are influenced by whether we feel we deserve to be fulfilled, or deprived. In satisfying our partners' needs, we see our own as being satisfied; and the greater the pleasure we give, the greater the pleasure we see ourselves as receiving.

Hence, the more undermining, intolerant, rejecting, critical, angry, hateful, treacherous, unloving or unwilling to forgive we may be toward others, the more so we tend to be toward ourselves. By the same token, the more supportive, tolerant, accepting, approving, compassionate, kind, honourable or willing to extend love and forgiveness we are, the more so we tend to be toward ourselves.

Finally, the causes for which we fight in life can often reflect unresolved causes within ourselves. Where we fight against what we see as injustices in society, we can be motivated by our own experiences of injustice in the past, or even by subconscious mental images of having *been* unjust sometime, for which we are attempting to compensate. This last point demonstrates how the sense of guilt in us can cause neural pathways to be created, which then spur us on to right the wrongs of the world.

SUMMARY

- ♣ Everyone and everything reflects some aspect of your nature to you.
- ♣ The beauty you see in others is a reflection of the beauty in yourself.
- ♣ The way you treat others is a reflection of how you feel you should be treated.

Recognise your reflections

1 If you have ever fought against, or supported, an injustice, can you:
   a) recall ever being a victim of a similar injustice?
   b) recall ever committing a similar injustice?
   c) trace any such injustice in your nature?

2 Which of the following reflect aspects of your nature to you? Choose as many as appropriate.
   a) Making your living:
      Shark. Octopus. Cuckoo. Sponge. Leech. Tiger. Rhinoceros. Jackal. Hawk. Bee. Dove. Fountain.
   b) Relating with others:
      Bull. Rhinoceros. Rottweiler. Snake. Wasp. Rabbit. Cat. Labrador. Dove.
   c) Expressing yourself:
      Drum. Trumpet. Cymbal. Violin. Flute. Triangle.
   d) Passing your life:
      Ocean. River. Lake. Pond. Stream.

3 What can you learn to your advantage from someone you know:
   a) whom you like or admire?
   b) whom you dislike or resent, if any?

4 Of these two puppies in need:
   a) for which do you have greater sympathy?
   b) with which do you more honestly identify?

Constantly look for your reflections in others.

CHAPTER SEVEN

Betrayal and Trust

During the Roman Empire, Androcles, a Christian, had taken refuge in a forest, when he encountered a lion attempting to flee from hunters. Drawing closer, Androcles saw that the lion was limping. Without concern for himself, he approached the lion and drew out a thorn that had implanted itself in one of its paws. Vowing that if it could ever return the favour it would do so, the lion escaped.

Years later Androcles found himself in an arena with other Christians, about to be devoured by lions. As the doors of the lions' cages opened, one of the lions bounded toward him. As fate would have it, this was the very same lion that Androcles had saved many years before. 'Lion ...' Androcles exclaimed with great relief, '... you remember me! I'm the one who helped you escape many years ago.'

There are two versions of the end to this tale. One version is that when the lion recognised Androcles, it honoured its word and spared his life. The other is that it replied: 'Yes, but that was a long time ago. What have you done for me *recently*?' and, at that, it ate Androcles.

The bridges of life

In life, everything we achieve and every penny we possess is the result of energy with which others have provided us, directly or indirectly, recently or long ago. That energy may be through their actions, the love they showed, the wars they fought, the countries they built, or the sanctuaries, introductions, undertakings, services, jobs or other opportunities they provided. It may be through what they have sold us that in turn enabled us to profit in some way, or, simply, through their presence. It may even be through the paths they showed us to avoid ... at their own cost. Prisons are brimming over with people, but for whom, many of us would be there! However it manifests itself, that energy creates 'bridges', which enable us to advance from where we were before, to where we are now. Do you appreciate the bridges with which others have provided you, or do you take those bridges for granted?

Reciprocation vs. betrayal

If there is one pattern of behaviour that can resolve the conflicts on this planet, that pattern is 'reciprocation'. And if there is one that can only escalate that conflict, it is 'betrayal'. The more we all genuinely reciprocate one another's goodwill and respect one another's interests as if they were our own, the greater will be the harmony and accord in society. When there is no longer any betrayal, *all conflict on this planet will cease* and harmony and accord will replace it.

Why do we betray?

We betray when the neural pathways that prompt self-serving patterns of behaviour in us are stronger than those that prompt higher, more evolved patterns. The situations in which this occurs can range from the relatively minor, day-to-day ones, to those that contribute to the major conflicts in society and, ultimately, the world.

Do you ever smile when you don't mean what that smile conveys; make promises or agreements with the intention of breaking them if this becomes expedient; conveniently forget favours or hospitality that has been shown to you; pass judgements without having all the facts; exploit the primitive instincts of people, animals, or other creatures?

Do you indoctrinate or exploit those who are weak, less intelligent or aware; make others appear wrong when you know they are right; justify your actions to gain something to which you are not entitled; scheme to profit from others' misfortune; induce others to make decisions you know to be to their disadvantage; or leave others to bear the consequences of your actions?

In short, do you misuse your power, strength or authority for personal gain?

Let us look at some typical primitive patterns by which we might all betray one another.

Betrayal through misleading intentions

Betrayal is doing anything that others allow on trust, but that they would not have allowed if our intentions had been made known beforehand. In agreements, for instance, the consideration is not what was agreed, but what would have been agreed if all the facts had been known, beforehand.

In the jungles of Asia and South America are various species of firefly. Fireflies attract their mates by glowing on and off, as if in Morse code, each code being unique to its own species. Among these fireflies is a variety known as 'Photuris', which preys on other species. It does this by imitating their codes, which they interpret as invitations to mate. As they respond, *on trust*, Photuris pounces.

Betrayal through broken agreements

When we make agreements, we offer foundations upon which others construct their futures. Relying on those foundations, they perhaps make agreements with others, who, in turn, relying on them, make agreements with yet others and so on, all constructing their futures upon the original foundations we provided. When we break our agreements, we remove the foundations on which others have relied, on trust, which can bring about untold consequences and even ruin on countless people, of which we will never know.

When others trust us, they hand us power that we could not otherwise have. If they hand us that power because we have led them to believe they can trust us with it, using it against them is 'betrayal'.

Trustworthy behaviour is a pattern that differentiates the civilised human from the barbarian. In civilised society there is an understanding that we may all roam about freely, on condition that we abide by time-honoured codes of trust. We trust that we will not harm one another, steal one another's property, deceive one another and so on. Yet, after a thousand years of civilisation in almost every culture on this planet, that trust continues to be betrayed.

Passing unjust judgements on others is a common example of betrayal. Exaggerating the advantages of what we sell, concealing its disadvantages, or trying to sell what we suspect to be unsuitable for our customers are other examples. Having concern for their best interests and treating them as we would wish to be treated, on the other hand, are examples of 'trust'.

Betrayal through groundless judgements

One reason for passing judgements on others is to make ourselves seem worthier than we truly believe we are. The more inferior we make them appear, in our eyes or the eyes of others, the more superior we feel this makes us, particularly if they are famous, powerful or important. Another reason can be to justify what suits us. Wasps sting, for instance, so they are 'bad'. Bees sting too. But *they* give us honey. So they are 'good'.

We tend to judge as 'guilty' people accused, or simply suspected, of offences for which they have not yet been tried. We also tend to pass judgements on them according to their appearance, backgrounds, where or with whom they are seen, or what we hear about them ... later to find them to be 'really nice', or 'really interesting'. We often tend to look for the bad points in people rather than the good, or brand them 'worthless', 'cheap' or 'easy', without considering their circumstances, loneliness or hopes of finding love.

One ground for the judgements we pass tends to be the presumption that whoever seems to be the same as others, *is* the same, or must have the same nature. So we speak of 'that kind of man', 'that kind of woman' and 'those kinds of people'. In this way we constantly distance ourselves from — and betray — many good people who may be dissimilar to us in certain ways, yet whose natures may be no less noble than our own.

Betrayal through theft and lies

When someone devotes effort to a venture, the benefit he or she generates is a reserve of energy. This reserve might be in the form of money, property, information, knowledge, ideas and so on. If he or she then makes that reserve available to others, it becomes a bridge by which they can reach toward success. When it is used without consent, it is *theft*.

Lying is also theft, because in the lie there is the intention to have what it might not be possible to acquire if the truth were known. When we speak, the implied request is: 'Accept what I say, because *I* am saying it.' In return, the respondent is saying: 'I accept what you say, because I trust *you*.' In the lie there is a breach of that trust.

A lie is any statement that is intended to mislead. The ways in which it is possible to do so are boundless. They can range from statements that are plainly untrue to the more subtle that are intentionally ambiguous, confusing or illusory, or omit certain facts to cause inaccurate inferences to be drawn.

Here are 12 common forms of lie. Do you use any of these, perhaps in different ways?

The lie	**The truth**
• 'I will repay you.'	No intention to pay.
• 'Factory prices …'	The prices are retail, not trade.
• 'Up to 90% off …'	But mostly 1% off.
• 'Only 99p.'	Effectively £1.
• 'With pure x. '	But with hardly any pure x.

• 'My dog won't eat anything but x.'	Nothing but x was given to him.
• 'Probably the largest …'	But actually one of the smallest.
• 'A stone's throw from the sea.'	But actually on top of a cliff.
• 'In tests, nine out of ten preferred …'	The tests were on chosen subjects.
• 'Freshly cut …'	But freshly cut on another day.
• 'Home made …'	Whose home?
• 'Sorry I'm late. I was caught in a jam.'	But the jam was on another day.

The Wolf and the Lamb

A lamb was drinking beside a stream. Upstream was a wolf. Turning to the lamb the wolf snarled, 'I'm going to kill you now.' 'Why?' bleated the lamb. 'Because you're muddying my drinking water,.' the wolf replied. 'I cannot be muddying your drinking water, Sir …' the lamb reasoned respectfully, '… since you are upstream and I am downstream.' 'Well, you muddied it a year ago,' retorted the wolf. *'Sir'*, bleated the lamb, *'I'm only six months old'*. 'Then it was your father,' the wolf snapped impatiently and at that devoured the lamb.

Lies disguised as self-justification

Have you ever wanted something to which you were not entitled and then concocted some moral ground to justify having it? Has anyone ever extended some form of goodwill to you, or provided you with a 'bridge', which you did not later want to acknowledge? To justify not acknowledging it, did you then dismiss its value or, like Androclese's lion, find fault with the person? Have you ever held onto a position like a bulldog, even when you were wrong, or blamed someone else, when the fault was really yours? If your car is in collision with another car, is your first reaction to search for some way to see if the other driver is in the wrong?

In your differences with others, do you tend to show yourself right and them wrong? Is your community, political party or nation right and others wrong? Is your religion right and others wrong? Are those you love right and others wrong? If your pet squabbles with your neighbour's pet, is *your* pet right and your neighbour's wrong?

There can be no end to the convoluted arguments that we are capable of contriving to prove ourselves right, or to justify our actions, irrespective of the cost to others, or ourselves. Proving ourselves right can be more dear to us than our relationships, our success, our health and, sometimes, even our lives.

Do you know anyone who says, 'That's my opinion and I'm *wrong*'? Why is it so important to appear right? What reward does appearing right ultimately bring?

Appearing right implies a deservingness to be acknowledged, respected and approved of, all of which are tributaries of the one great ocean of need in every human being ... to be loved.

Here are seven common situations and typical statements by which some of us try to make ourselves appear right, or justify our behaviour at the expense of others. Don't take this too seriously, but see if any is familiar to you?

Underpaying the correct price for something:
- 'That's just my good luck.'
- 'I'm not responsible for their mistakes.'
- 'They make too much/enough profit anyway.'

Parking obstructively, or disregarding traffic codes:
- 'I'm late/won't be long.'

Not assisting the police or others who protect us:
- 'It's not my problem.'
- 'I don't like to get involved.'

Making no effort to help those in need:
- 'I have more pressing problems.'
- 'Charity begins at home.'

Trying to steal someone's partner:
- 'It's up to him/her.'
- 'They aren't happy anyway.'
- 'All's fair in love and war.'

Cheating, exploiting or stealing from someone:
- 'That's business/my job.'
- 'Others have done the same to me, or would if they could.'
- 'I've been wronged by someone of his/her occupation, community, nationality (or other category).'
- 'My ancestors were wronged by his/her ancestors.'

Engaging in or encouraging callousness to animals:
- 'I'm rendering a service to society.'
- 'It's better for them to die that way.'
- 'They do the same to each other.'
- 'They don't feel pain as we do.'
- 'They have to die sometime.'
- 'They're bred for it.'
- 'They deserve it.'
- 'They're there for us.
- 'God commanded us to do it'.

Identify betrayal

Here are ten theoretical scenarios. Answer 'yes' or 'no' to the question, *'Is this betrayal?'*. The question is not whether the action is understandable, justifiable, or common practice, but simply whether you see any *betrayal* in it. At the end, add up your totals.

1 Someone invites an acquaintance home for dinner. The acquaintance brings along a friend. The friend then engages in a secret relationship with the host's/hostess's partner. *Is this betrayal?*

2 A company has an arrangement where its employees take their wages out of a safe each week, according to their agreed rates of pay. An employee discovers that he receives less pay than others for the same work. So he takes the difference in addition to his agreed pay. *Is this betrayal?*

3 An employee leaves his job and takes the addresses of the employer's customers, to use at the next job. *Is this betrayal?*

4 A broker introduces a business contact to a prospective buyer. When the two meet, they discover they are old acquaintances. They then conclude a deal between themselves and reduce the broker's commission without his agreement. *Is this betrayal?*

5 An antiques dealer offers to sell an old-looking item to a customer, who asks its age. The dealer replies, factually, 'Under 100 hundred years old'. In fact, it is brand new. *Is this betrayal?*

6 Unaware of its rarity, someone takes an antique to a dealer for sale and agrees to let the dealer set a fair price for it. Knowing of its rarity, the dealer tells the owner it is not valuable and sets a lower price than the owner would have accepted if he/she had known the truth. *Is this betrayal?*

7 Someone takes a bet with another, knowing it is *impossible* for that person to win. *Is this betrayal?*

8 Someone visits a company on business and is served efficiently by an employee. Sometime later he/she sees the employee in the street and offers him/her a job. *Is this betrayal?*

9 Someone lends a sum of money to another who does not repay it by the promised time, even though he can. The lender then borrows something of equal value from him, undertaking to return it the next day. He then announces that he intends to retain it until the debt is repaid. *Is this betrayal?*

10 A motorist is waiting while someone leaves a parking space. Before he has time to take it, another motorist, who has not been waiting, darts in and takes it. *Is this betrayal?*

11 During the 16th Century, two swordsmen are engaged in a duel to the death, when one of them drops his sword. The other lowers his own sword to allow him to pick it up. He picks it up and while the other's is still lowered, runs him through. *Is this betrayal?*

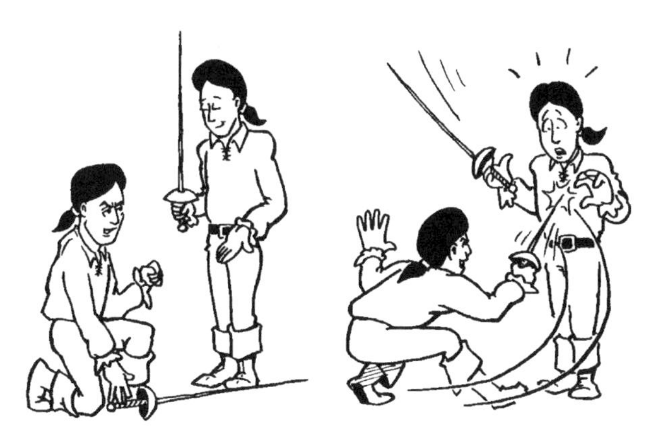

Add up your totals. The higher your 'yes' total, the higher your level of integrity. The higher your 'no' total … well, you decide!

Acknowledge Betrayal

1 Recall an occasion, if any, when you tried to prove yourself right, when you were not.
   a) What did you hope to gain by doing this?
   b) Did you acknowledge it later? If not, why not?

2 Recall an occasion when you were misjudged.
   a) On what evidence was that misjudgement based?
   b) Were you given an opportunity to defend yourself?
   c) How did you feel about that?

3 Recall an occasion when you passed a judgement on someone.
   a) On what evidence did you base your judgement?
   b) Are you certain your judgement was well-founded?
   c) Did you give that person an opportunity to defend himself or herself? If not, why not?

4 Recall a recent occasion when you broke an agreement with someone.
   a) How do you feel about that now?
   b) Would you do it again? If so, why?

5 Recall a recent occasion when you kept an agreement, or otherwise behaved honourably, even when it was inconvenient to do so.
   a) How do you feel about that?
   b) Would you do the same again?
   If not, why not?

6 Recall a financial transaction in which you were involved.
   a) Did you care about the other person's interests?
   b) If not, would you have felt better if you had?
   c) Would you be willing to care about others' interests in the future? If not, why not?

7 Which of these situations represents you more?

SUMMARY

- Everything you achieve in life can be attributed to bridges with which others have provided you.
- When others trust you, they give you power that you could not otherwise have.
- When you make agreements, you provide foundations on which others construct their futures.
- The principal cause of all conflict is betrayal.
- Respecting others' needs and reciprocating goodwill are two keys to resolving all conflict on the planet.

Constantly be aware of the agreements you make and how others may be affected by them.

CHAPTER EIGHT

The Sense of Guilt

Do you ever feel guilty simply because you think you *ought* to feel that way, even about the slightest thing ... not sending greetings cards, for instance? If you achieve something without much effort, do you feel you don't deserve the reward when it comes? Do you make life as difficult as possible for yourself, or keep putting obstacles in your own way, to ensure you *do* deserve it?

As a child, did you ever try to make others feel guilty if they didn't do what you wanted, by crying, *'You don't love me, if you really loved me you'd...'*? Do you perhaps use the same sort of manipulation on others now, in your adulthood?

Depending on our upbringing, we all tend to suffer to varying degrees from feelings of guilt, for what we have or have not done in the past, in relation to parents, children, peers, religion and so on. These feelings (which may at times be accurate, but are often are groundless) are determined by the beliefs we hold as to what is 'right' or 'wrong'. When those close to us die, for instance, we tend to feel we should have done more for them when they were alive and judge ourselves for what we did *not* do, rather than for what we did.

The mechanism for this sense of guilt is in the neurons of

the brain. Just as, when they detect malfunctions in our physical systems, they prompt us to rectify them by causing physical pain, when they detect malfunctions in our *thinking processes* or *behaviour*, they cause us emotional pain, or the 'sense of guilt'.

Origins of the sense of guilt

As our ancestors evolved over the last few thousand years, they cultivated codes of duty and of justice. The reward for adhering to those codes was the right to enjoy the pleasures and benefits of their respective societies. However, that right carried with it a caveat, which was that if they breached those codes, they no longer deserved those rewards. This is how the principle of 'right' and 'wrong' evolved in the neural pathways of our ancestors. So now, when we feel we have breached any of those codes, we believe we do not deserve what we desire. The result is the sense of guilt.

Sense of guilt, or actual guilt?

It does not necessarily follow, simply because we sense we are guilty, that we are actually guilty. It is therefore important to differentiate between the *sense* of guilt and *actual* guilt.

The *sense* of guilt occurs when our neurons tell us we have breached certain codes, or failed to fulfil certain duties, based on our beliefs as to what we 'should' or 'should not' have done. On the other hand, *actual* guilt is a fact. In other words, if we *have* breached certain codes, or failed in certain duties, we *are* guilty. So whereas *actual* guilt is based on *fact*, the *sense* of it is based only on *belief*.

We obviously have certain duties, such as toward those

who supported us caringly during our formative years and of course toward the societies in which we choose to live. However, it does not necessarily follow that simply because we *believe* we have those duties, they actually exist. We can be misguided, or indoctrinated into believing we have these, when we do not.

Levels of consciousness, levels of guilt

If the cat eats the canary, or the puppy soils the carpet, is it guilty? Is the cuckoo guilty for laying an egg in a nest that another bird has built, or her fledglings guilty for forcing out another bird's young? Is the predator of the jungle guilty for eating its prey alive, the mosquito for drinking our blood, the rat for spreading disease, or the virus for invading our bodies?

Creatures of lower levels of consciousness do not understand anything about codes of behaviour and duty. So in them there can be no guilt. However, we humans, with our high levels of consciousness, do understand. So our failure to observe those codes *is* guilt. The levels of that guilt correspond to the levels of our consciousness and so, the levels of our understanding … the higher the levels, the greater the guilt.

Once again, however, just as it does not necessarily follow that because we *feel* guilty, we *are* guilty, it does not follow that because we *do not*, we *are not*. In the same way that we can turn on the switches along our neural pathways to induce the sense of guilt in ourselves, we can turn them off to shut down that sense, so as to be able to justify certain behaviour. Killing, cheating, violating and disregarding the feelings of people and creatures are examples of such behaviour.

Levels of duty

Duties may be said to occur at three levels. The most elementary level, of course, is where there is an agreement to do or not do something. A higher level is where no agreement has been made, but where there is an understanding that something will or will not be done. An example of this would be in behaving toward someone in a noble way, on the assumption that he or she will reciprocate the same spirit.

Beyond these two levels may be said to be a higher level still. That level concerns those with whom it is not possible to enter into any agreement, or to have any understanding. The very young, the unintelligent and those of the animal world would fall into this category. This means, for instance, that those of us who eat creatures, have the 'higher-consciousness duty' to ensure that they experience no fear or suffering beforehand.

Agreements with ourselves

Sometimes, we can fail to fulfil agreements we have made with ourselves. This can occur, for instance, where we have set ourselves certain standards of behaviour, based on duties we believe we have. Although those standards may have come to us from our own higher consciousness, or even from some higher dimension, we could just as easily have fabricated them as a result of misguided assumptions, or indoctrination by others. The biblical exhortation *'An eye for an eye'* and the injunction *'No sex outside marriage'* are two examples, which have caused incalculable misery in certain societies. However they occur, if we fail to meet the standards we have set ourselves, we induce the sense of shame, or guilt, in ourselves.

The self-punishment entanglement

When something undesirable happens to you, do you ask yourself: *'What have I done to deserve this?'*

When we believe we deserve to be rewarded, we turn on the switches along our pathways that urge us to feel great. Then we exude confidence, charisma and joy and success follows us wherever we go. However, even though we may consciously strive for success or fulfilment in various ways, if we believe we are guilty, even on account of events of long ago, we can subconsciously devise ways to sabotage ourselves; like pressing down on the brake and accelerator pedals at the same time, when motoring.

The extent to which we are capable of doing this should not be underestimated. It can range from simply depriving ourselves of what we desire in the short term, to doing so for our entire lives. As we manage to overcome some of the devices we have set up to deprive ourselves in one way, we might plan other devices to defeat ourselves in others, further ahead. These can be emotional devices, or even *fortresses*, to blockade ourselves from the love we desire, for instance, preventing not only others from reaching in to us, but ourselves from reaching out to them.

We can apply the sense of guilt and self-punishment to ourselves to varying degrees, like turning a 'guilt-intensity'

dial higher or lower, according to the intensity of our perceived guilt.

This perception and the devices we set up can then eventually entangle us, leaving us with no apparent means of escape.

Sources of the sense of guilt

In addition to the pathways that prompt the sense of guilt in us, there can be many other sources, each tugging us in its own direction.

One source, which affects us to lesser or greater degrees throughout our lives, can be our parents' attitudes as to what is 'wrong' or 'sinful' (which may or may not be accurate). Another can be any sense of guilt that our parents inherited, which some psychologists now believe is in turn transmitted genetically to the children. Yet another source can be other people, from whom we adopt various beliefs in life ... some rational, valid and constructive; others, irrational, antisocial and destructive, both to ourselves and others.

Although the subject of Chapter 12, there are two other possible sources that deserve mention here. These are the periods during *previous* physical lifetimes and the periods *between* those lifetimes in the non-physical dimension, where we might acquire higher codes of behaviour. Recorded in our memory systems, these codes, if they conflict with any lower behaviour or intentions, might then create some sense of guilt.

Establish the facts

If you feel any sense of guilt, it is important to be clear as to whether you are *factually* guilty, or simply *feel* guilty, without any valid justification for it. This you can do only through detached, honest and objective reasoning. Check whether it is because you have *actually* breached any of society's codes, or failed in any duty, or simply because others say you are guilty. If the latter, are they expressing opinions that they adopted from others, or do they have *factual* evidence for saying so?

If you decide you are not factually guilty, the matter is at an end ... unless you enjoy the feeling, in which case you will never be short of things to feel guilty about. If you decide you *are* factually guilty, on the other hand, follow the process of release on page 98.

Following this, your brain should discontinue conveying messages that you do not deserve what you desire. Any devices you have set up to deprive yourself of what you desire should then become eliminated, leaving you free to enjoy a greater sense of your true worth, the fulfilment of your needs, respect, love and a happier life. This will in turn open the way for the development of the highest aspects of your nature and the fullest possible expression of your excellence, inner beauty and love.

As you can see, in moderation, the sense of guilt is essential, because it can help modify any lower, antisocial inclinations and turn off the switches along the neural pathways that prompt them. In excess, however, it can be counter-productive and destructive, preventing you from enjoying your due fulfilment in life and any higher purpose for which you have been born.

SUMMARY

- ♣ Your sense of guilt is determined by the beliefs you hold and prompts you to correct your thinking or behaviour.
- ♣ The solution to any unjustified sense of guilt is to recognise it as such and to release yourself.

Recognise the sense of guilt

1 Recall a time when you tried to please someone.
   a) What expectation were you trying to fulfil in him or her?
   b) Would you have felt guilty if you had not?

2 Recall a time when you tried to manipulate someone into pleasing you.
   a) What expectation did you want him or her to fulfil in you?
   b) Did you want him or her to feel guilty if he or she did not?

3 Recall a time when you:
   a) felt guilty when you were not guilty.
   b) felt guilty when you *were* guilty.
   Do you recognise the difference in these feelings?

4 Consider a time when, in your opinion, you were actually guilty of something.
   a) Have you ceased feeling guilty about it?
   b) If not, are you willing to do so?
   c) If not, why not … and how long do you intend to continue doing so, or until what occurs?

Constantly be aware of the underlying causes of any guilt you feel and the ways in which it drives you.

CHAPTER NINE

Unfulfilled Expectations

You may know people who habitually speak in hostile tones, criticise others or complain about them.

When we are angry about the past, what we feel, think, say and do is affected by that anger in everyday life, through the intonations of our voices, the words we choose, our postures, our subtle facial expressions and the look in our eyes. However, when we neutralise the causes of that anger, these become infused with warmth, humour, love and other higher aspects of our nature.

There is a difference between *having* the faculty of anger and being *ruled* by it. Though anger is useful in certain situations, if you constantly feel angry, a little insight into the possible causes will be helpful toward reducing the persistent mental images that accompany the anger and the sometimes debilitating charge that is generated.

Disappointment and anger

Essentially, the cause of anger is rooted in a sense of disappointment at expectations not being fulfilled. When we fear that certain situations are going to occur, for instance, images of those situations appear in our minds, causing charges to surge along our 'fight or flight' pathways, in preparation for any response that may prove necessary.

These 'fight or flight' pathways began to evolve millions of years ago when we, or rather, our reptilian ancestors, fought their enemies and ate them, or took flight and survived. When we later discover, or *believe*, that those situations are not going to occur, the charges cease, the images fade, our systems 'stand down' and we experience that sense of relief, or 'peace'.

Likewise, when we expect certain *desirable* situations to occur, later to discover or believe that they will not be realised, the same pathways become activated, in readiness to rectify the situations. The greater our expectations were, the more aggressive our 'fight' responses become. The emotion we then feel is 'anger'.

Obviously, no charge is generated when we *expect* to fail and we fail, because there is no disappointment to cause this. Soldiers injured on the battlefield do not experience the same intensity of anger as civilians injured in the street, for instance, because unlike civilians, they *have* expectations of being injured.

It follows then, that the fewer the expectations you hold, the less charge you will generate and the less disappointment or anger you will experience. Remember this when things don't go as you want!

Powerlessness and rage

Have you ever driven down a street in a tearing hurry, to discover it closed off ... and there was no sign to warn you? Have you ever wanted something desperately, but couldn't have it because of someone's obstinacy...and time was running out? Have you ever felt let down by someone at the last moment, or felt cheated or betrayed ... and powerless to bring the offender to justice? Have you ever tried to destroy something, or prevent someone else having something that had eluded you ... because if you couldn't have it, *no-one* would?

When you are in situations that you feel powerless to

change, or from which you feel powerless to escape, do you feel enraged ... even just a little? Rage is the sudden surge of charge, generated to deal with unexpected predicaments and finding no outlet through which to become channelled. At that moment the mind is so occupied with the predicament, that there is nothing else in view. Hence the term 'blind rage'.

Nor is our rage necessarily caused by those to whom we direct it. It may be caused by others who are inaccessible, or whom we fear, or who simply remind us of those who *are* the causes. It may even be caused — and this should not be overlooked — by ourselves, on account of what we have done or failed to do, contrary to expectations we have of ourselves.

The death of those we love can sometimes arouse such intense rage that we then fall into the common pattern of blaming it on others. That our opportunities of enjoying certain fulfilments in life are fading, is another common cause of rage. In our considering the possibility that those opportunities may be available to us again in some future lifetime, however, this rage may diminish, or even evaporate entirely.

Childhood memories, adult rage

When we cry or laugh, images of what pains or confuses us appear in our minds; each exhalation being an attempt to expel the charge generated through those images. During childhood, much of the charge generated through painful experiences is channelled-out through crying (now a recognised therapy for the reduction of stress). Where memories of such experiences persist into adulthood, however, the neurons continue to generate some charge on their account.

Overlooking the fact that our parents were once children

too, with their own hopes, struggles, painful experiences and unfulfilled needs, many of us tend to blame them for failing to live up to our expectations, or to provide the love or fulfilment that *we* needed in our earlier years.

However adult in physical years we may be, we all regress from time to time to various 'emotional ages'. Those ages relate to emotionally charged, 'enraging' episodes in our childhood, recorded in the archives of our memories. Whenever similar situations occur later in life, they cause memories of the earlier events to erupt into our minds, arousing precisely the same emotions — and rage — as at those earlier times.

Rejection and revenge

The experiences of fulfilment and disappointment during our early years are the building blocks upon which our adulthood is constructed; acceptance and rejection being the most critical.

Of all the causes of rage, one of the most intolerable, particularly during adolescence and early adulthood, is powerlessness at not having our loving or sexual needs fulfilled. When thwarted, the rage that results can create responses in the oldest networks of the brain, driving the relentless quest for the fulfilment of those needs. Sometimes, this can be at tremendous cost, both to ourselves and to others. So much so, some people will slave, enslave, cheat, steal, exploit, fight, kill, betray friends, waste fortunes, go to prison and even die for it.

Of course, everyone has the right to try to attract partners to themselves and to accept or reject whoever responds. However, for an harmonious society to exist, those who have the power to attract others sexually, need to be sensitive to the silent rage that can be generated through 'rejection' and to moderate their powers in public places with appropriate discretion.

Aggression, a channel of expression

During adulthood, when emotionally charged memories relating to parents or anyone else come to mind, the neurons generate some charge on their account, even though we may not be conscious of it. This results in the sense of rage, which *must* be expressed somehow.

According to the intensity of the charge, this rage may express itself through constantly complaining about situations and people, vandalising property, cheating, bullying, rioting, oppression, cruelty, abuse of humans and animals and other, multifarious forms of antisocial behaviour. The demand for violent films and video games, which provide channels of expression for this rage, the tremendous attendance at boxing matches and the expressions on the faces of spectators baying for more, are evidence of this rage seeking expression.

However the rage is expressed, the need that underlies it is for the love and caring for which the 'inner child' of earlier years still yearns. Even if its original cause may be forgotten consciously, so long as the charge continues to be generated, the 'inner child' continues subconsciously to express his or her unfulfilled need to be loved throughout adulthood, one way or another.

Some people, aware of the consequences of their rage expressing itself in aggressive ways, refrain from cultivating their physical strength, so as to prevent its expression. In contrast, there are those who, if they do not receive the respect, love, sexual fulfilment or material benefits that they see others enjoying, will deliberately cultivate their physical strength, so as to be able to take 'revenge' against those who they feel are responsible; and to inflict the same intensity of pain on them as they are enduring. Hence the familiar expressions, *'getting even'*, making others *'pay for it'* and not letting them *'get away with it'*. And because the most intense pain is experienced through those we love, the need for revenge against them can often be that much greater.

Intentions underlying aggression

It is important to recognise that underlying an act of aggression, there can also be the subconscious intention to kill. We know, for instance, that in striking something fragile, such as a watch, we intend to destroy it. In striking a person, therefore, there *can* be the subconscious intention to destroy that person. By the same token, then, in creating, promoting or even allowing a situation where *oneself* is struck, there can be the subconscious intention to be punished for something over which one feels guilty.

Harbours of suppressed rage

Ships anchored in a harbour and laden with missiles are useful metaphors for inner rage. The more repressed the rage, the more explosive the eventual release or 'outburst' can be. At any time, these ships can slip out to sea to

release their charge. Some may be great battleships, causing gigantic waves and wreaking havoc in otherwise calm waters. Others may be submarines, sneaking up on their unsuspecting quarries. Many may remain quietly at anchor for years, accumulating their determination for revenge ... their dreadful potential unbeknown to anyone, including, possibly, even themselves.

Imaginary adversaries

Ten thousand years ago our ancestors passed their lives sleeping, searching for food and procreating. As they evolved, they learned to eat one another, steal one another's food — and partners — invade one another's territories and defend their own. Such are some of the primitive patterns that have been transmitted from generation to generation up to the present time.

Nowadays, when we invade territories, or commit some form of physical aggression, five possible underlying needs will be: to retrieve what we believe belongs to us; take what does not; prove our worth; give expression to our 'warring' or 'killing' pathways; and destroy those we regard as our adversaries.

This last need may not be not as obvious as it appears, however. These 'adversaries' ... do they always *actually* exist, or do they sometimes exist only in our minds?

Dungeons of the mind

You may have noticed people walking along the street,

muttering angrily at others in their imagination, invisible to you, but very real to them. Perhaps you do this too. Young boys can be seen in playgrounds, pretending to shoot at imaginary enemies. If you practise martial arts, shadow-boxing or workouts in the gym, perhaps, in your mind, you hold an image of someone with whom you are 'getting even'.

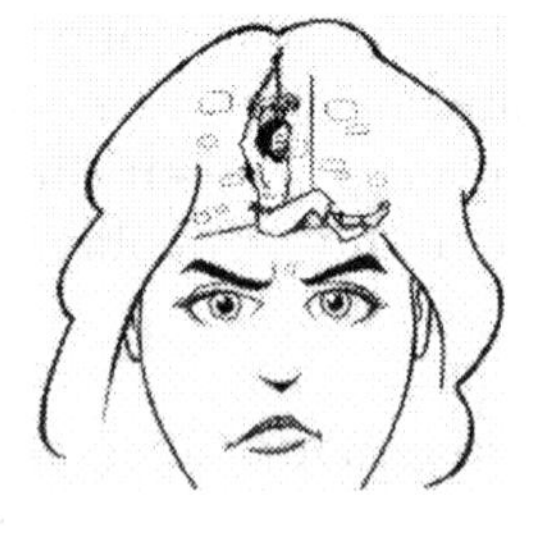

When we behave aggressively toward others, whether physically or verbally, it is not necessarily they who are in our minds at those moments. It may be others from the past who we feel have offended or betrayed us, or those we love. It may even be *ourselves*, on account of past actions, or aspects of our nature, for which we feel guilty.

Because we cannot get at the actual offenders, or at ourselves, our neurons generate charges that maintain images of them, or of ourselves, in the respective situations, in our minds. It is as if we then keep them locked in 'mental dungeons', where we punish them, or hold them secure until they can be brought to some 'higher justice' later.

Punishing offenders through substitutes

Meantime, powerless to exact this justice, we channel our rage through 'substitutes', whom we encounter from day to day. These may be competitors in business, opponents in sport (whom we speak of beating and thrashing) victims of road rage or other acts of violence, people, animals or other creatures we violate, people we cheat or from whom we steal, or those who simply bear the brunt of our discourteous remarks. Very often, these are people who are the most easily accessible to us ... those we love.

Whatever we do to the substitutes, until we have neutralised the *causes* of the images appearing in our minds, they continue to present themselves, even while we sleep. Thus, those with whom we relate from day to day, become innocent 'conductors', through whom we channel the surges of charge generated in response to others' behaviour, life's predicaments or simply ourselves.

The deleterious effects of these images

Any charge constantly generated through hatred, envy, resentment, jealousy or sense of guilt, even though subconsciously, causes reactions in the body as it courses through it. The body goes into a state of 'fight or flight', the facial muscles draw back to bare the teeth as a warning, the scalp and ear muscles tense up, adrenaline, hormones and other trace elements enter the bloodstream and hydrochloric acid and enzymes are released into the stomach to digest the 'vanquished' enemies (all of which animals can detect through our pores and breath). Over and above this, like lightning out of storm-laden skies, the charge may 'discharge' itself forcibly, through outbursts of rage, or other intemperate behaviour.

Release the images

Well, what is the solution? Clearly, it's not to ignore the images that infiltrate our minds. That would be to ignore possibly invaluable warning signals. Nor is it to suppress them with alcohol or drugs ... or indeed, to require that others make allowances for us all our lives. No, the solution must be to acknowledge the images, recognise those that are without foundation, or that relate to ancient threats that are now obsolete and then to 'release' them, as we shall see in the following chapter.

To be able to do this, however, there must be the willingness to renounce any further intention to punish the people, *or yourself*, represented by the images that appear. Then the charge generated to maintaining them will cease and your mind will become free.

Following this, any action you take against anyone, will not be out of any desire for revenge, but only to reinstate what is legitimately yours, or to achieve compliance with the law. Then you will find yourself with improved health, increased energy for more productive tasks, in greater harmony with everyone with whom you relate and, most importantly, at peace.

Understanding your sense of rage

1. Recall a time when you directed your anger at someone who was not the actual cause of that anger.
   a) Who or what *was* the cause?
   b) Why did you direct it at that 'substitute'?

2. Recall a time when you directed your anger at someone who *was* the cause.
   a) What did you need from that person, for you to feel less angry?
   b) Are you willing to release him or her now? If not, why not?

3 Recall a time when you were, or wanted to be, aggressive toward someone.
  a) What did you want that person (or his or her substitute) to know?
  b) What did you want to receive from him or her?
  c) Are you willing to forgive him or her now? If not, why not?

4 Recall a time when you were rejected by someone:
  a) What judgement did you form about yourself?
  b) How could that person have rejected you in a more caring way?

5 Recall a time when you rejected someone (if there *is* anyone).
  a) What judgement do you think the person formed of himself or herself?
  b) How could you have rejected him or her in a more caring way?

6 Recall a time when you felt cheated or betrayed by someone.
  a) Are you harbouring any feeling of rage toward that person now?
  b) In the dungeon of your mind, are you holding or punishing him or her?
  c) If so, what benefit are you deriving from this?
  d) Are you willing to discontinue doing this? If not, why not?
  e) And if not, for how many hours, days, weeks, months or years do you intend to continue doing so?

7 Think of someone who enrages you (if there is anyone).
   a) What is the emotion you feel and where do you feel it?
   b) What judgement are you passing about that person?
   c) Think of that person again, this time taking a neutral position … that is to say, without any judgement.
   d) Do you still feel the same emotion?

8 In the dungeon of your mind:
   a) How many people (if any) are there?
   b) Are you there, too?
   c) How many are you willing to release?
   d) If not all, why not?

SUMMARY

- ♣ Initially, anger is the generation of charge, when one's hopes or expectations are not fulfilled.
- ♣ Persistent anger can be the intention to punish.
- ♣ Rage is the surge of charge generated at the sense of powerlessness.
- ♣ Violence is the attempt to punish or destroy the cause of the rage.

Constantly be aware of the underlying causes of any rage you feel and the ways in which they drive you.

CHAPTER TEN

Neutrality and Peace

One of the keys toward being at peace is achieving the state of 'neutrality'. Advocated in Buddhism, Taoism and Hinduism, being 'neutral' means being open to *what is* and *what is not*, irrespective of how you would have preferred a particular situation to be.

Of course, it is necessary for us to have hopes. It is also necessary to have expectations on which to plan the future. But the less you *rely* on a particular situation turning out as you wish (as to your rights, being accepted, respected or loved, life being trouble, accident or betrayal free, at work, at home, on the road, or anywhere else) the more toward 'neutral' you will become and the less disappointment or rage you will experience, when it does not.

Tolerance is not neutrality

Neutrality is not the same as tolerance. There is much to be said for being tolerant, of course. But unlike neutrality, which is the *willing openness* to a situation, tolerance is its *grudging acceptance.* When you are tolerant, your neurons continue to generate some charge to maintain mental images of what it is you are tolerating, producing subconscious annoyance, or pain, so long as those images persist. Although you may be able to remedy the situation, no amount of annoyance or pain will alter the fact that that situation *has* occurred.

Toward reaching the state of neutrality, it is necessary to:

- Ease the *rigidity* of your expectations.
- Acknowledge the truth about situations that annoy you.
- Cease habitually passing judgements in your mind.
- Be willing to forgive others and yourself, emotionally.

Cease passing judgements

If you habitually pass judgements in your mind, whether about others or yourself, ceasing doing so may not be so easy a task at first. With *intention*, however, this becomes increasingly easy the more you practice, until your pathways eventually cease prompting you to do so.

A technique you may wish to practice, to help you get out of the habit of passing these judgements, is to think of an injustice that has occurred toward yourself, society or elsewhere in the world. Then adopt a 'non-judgemental' position, so that you are aware of the injustice, but without the emotion of anger to accompany it ... in other words, having neutralised the emotion.

As you accomplish this, you will find the occasions for disappointment and rage diminishing. You will also find yourself more readily open to the facts of situations *as they actually are*, especially when disappointing, or 'outrageous' situations present themselves, as they do for all of us at times.

If you feel your trust has been betrayed, for instance, ask yourself whether you created, promoted or allowed this to occur. Did you fail to take the proper precautions? Perhaps you hadn't wanted to consider the possibility of being betrayed, because if you had, it would have meant you could not take a particular risk, which in turn would mean you could not get the benefit for which you were hoping. In short, did you *choose* not to look and thereby *choose* not to know?

If you are offended by someone's (or a parrot's) remark, check whether that remark concurs with some belief *you* hold about yourself, or conflicts with your need to be liked, or loved. If you are disappointed over a situation, check whether your expectations accord with the *realities* of that situation. More importantly, check whether your needs accord with the needs of others involved.

Let go and *win*

From time to time during your life, you no doubt hold certain positions 'on principle'. Those positions might involve arguing or complaining about causes that concern you, standing up for justice or moral issues, or proving yourself 'right' or 'innocent'. You might even make yourself a willing victim, or martyr, to be admired for your suffering.

To justify your position, you might protest that justice, or your moral values, must prevail at all cost. Rather than yield your position, you might then pursue the cause relentlessly for years, or the whole of your life, not only depleting your emotional reserves and physical system, but diverting valuable energy from what could be more productive and rewarding pursuits in your life.

Often, the truthful reason for holding these positions will be to appear worthy in your own eyes, or in the eyes of the world, because, in your mind, 'letting go' means 'losing'. But does it always mean 'losing', or can it sometimes mean abandoning useless baggage and 'winning' peace and good health?

In resisting the inclination to take up such positions,

even when you are right — in other words, adopting the position of neutrality instead — you may find that a particular issue over which you would normally fight, is not as important as you had been telling yourself, all along.

Play a game of neutrality

An entertaining way to cultivate neutrality is to play a card game, where you can see your opponent's hand, but where he or she cannot see yours. Play your hand as if you did not know what was in your opponent's hand. When you have succeeded in playing without regard for what you know, you have reached a higher level of neutrality. You have also reached a higher level of trustworthiness, integrity and consciousness.

Forgive and release others and yourself

The most important key toward achieving neutrality and peace is forgiveness ... of others and of yourself.

Forgiving others does not mean making them 'right'. It simply means releasing them *emotionally* for offences you feel they have committed. This means ceasing any anger toward them and having no further intention to punish them *out of anger*; although they may still be liable for any damage they have caused, or offences they have committed in law.

When you have released the image of someone, you may notice a reduction in tension somewhere in your body, through which some charge was flowing in support of your 'fight or flight' mechanism.

By the same token, forgiving yourself means releasing yourself emotionally for offences you feel you have committed. This means ceasing any anger toward yourself and having no further intention to punish yourself.

It is important also to recognise that self-forgiveness is not a device for absolving ourselves of duties we have neglected, damage we have not made good, or debts we have not discharged. Unless we truly intend to do so where we can, the sense of guilt will persist, because our brains know everything about us, including our intentions.

When fresh situations give rise to your feeling anger, pain or guilt, release the images *immediately*. Do not allow the feeling to run its usual course, otherwise it will contaminate what you think, feel, say and do.

When a violent scene is about to appear on television, switch over to another channel until you are sure it has passed. Don't be tempted to watch, otherwise you will reinforce the pathways that promote those feelings, or behaviour.

It is important to recognise that it is not open to us to forgive people for what they have done to others. Only those who have been affected can do so. We can only forgive them for what they have done to us.

Be patient

The full effect of this process will not necessarily be immediate. Some situations can take time before they are resolved entirely. There may also be many images to be released. But each time your brain recognises that you *genuinely intend* to release them, the intensity of charge generated to maintaining them will gradually diminish.

A suggested method, which I find helpful, to see whether you are still holding anyone in your 'mental dungeon', is to think: *'I forgive everyone for everything'*. If an image of someone appears, relating to what you see as betrayal, rejection, aggression, injustice, groundless judgement and so on, think to the image: *'I release you'*. Thereupon, it should disappear ... provided, of course, this is genuinely your intention. Genuine release means that images of believed offenders are no longer sufficiently charged, to be re-generated into the mind. If an image of someone does not disappear, repeat the 'release' statement until it does.

If a particular image persistently re-appears, however, there can be two reasons. The first is that through the process of association, it is being re-generated, because an aspect of that person's nature is stimulating some aspect of your own. That image would then be a signal to you of a pattern in yourself needing correction.

The second possible reason is that you have not genuinely intended the release. Hence the expression, *'I can forgive, but I can never forget'*. There can of course be situations where people are guilty of offences for which it seems unlikely that they will ever be brought to account, or where their offences are so grievous or persistent that we cannot bring ourselves to forgive them. Don't be annoyed with yourself if this is the case. It is sometimes difficult to succeed at first. Simply acknowledge your reason for holding the image *('I am holding the image of ...../myself, because I want to punish him/her/myself')*. Perhaps, in time, you will decide to discontinue doing so.

In the same way that you have released others, do the same for yourself, thinking: *'I forgive myself for everything'*. If an image of yourself in a particular situation constantly re-appears, it means you have not forgiven yourself. If this is the case, check whether you believe you would not repeat the same offence. If this is so and you have made all genuine efforts to make recompense where you can, forgiveness of yourself is justified. Therefore, say or think to the image in your mind: *' (Your name) I forgive you'*.

As you accustom yourself to performing this process as soon as such images appear, you will be surprised at the ease with which you are able to release them, even while you are occupied with other matters.

It is most important to recognise that this 'release' process is not one of suppressing images, or of ignoring them. Nor is it one of trying to convince yourself that you do not feel what you really do feel. It is one of *ceasing your intention to punish* others or yourself. It may help to remind yourself that the behaviour of others, as of yourself, is *always* due to promptings by neural pathways that have not yet been 'switched off'.

Nothing to forgive

As we have seen, there can be situations where we have passed judgements on others, when they are in fact innocent. This might be where we have had expectations of them that they have not fulfilled, for instance, or where, in retrospect, our feelings of anger were unreasonable, exaggerated or are simply no longer valid. In other words, there is really *nothing to forgive*. In that case, forgiveness is obviously not appropriate. If you find this to be so, just acknowledge the fact and 'release' the image.

Thorns in your heart

We have all had instances of being in love, perhaps long ago, with people who did not reciprocate our feelings. Some of us can carry the pain of those experiences around with us all our lives, like thorns in our hearts. These then serve as perpetual reminders of the love we felt. It is as if we can in this way convince them, or some 'higher observer', of the genuineness of our love and the injustice or suffering we have been enduring. And so we hold them, unjustly, in the dungeons of our minds, together with all the others who we feel have offended or betrayed us during our lives.

Hurting yourself to punish others

Are you angry with someone who you feel has caused you some disadvantage in life? If so, check whether you are subconsciously *perpetuating* that disadvantage, so as to be able to justify continuing to blame or even punish that person.

At an Insight seminar, some years ago, there was a young woman who had been involved in a motor accident, in which the other driver was at fault. She was dependent on crutches and quite naturally enraged at that person. During the seminar she recognised that she was maintaining her incapacity, so as to be able to blame the other driver. She then went through a process of forgiveness and release and at the end of that seminar she walked out unaided. To the best of my knowledge, she has done so perfectly well, ever since.

Cease the anger: neutrality and peace

The essential point is not to use anger, or self-induced pain, as a means of punishment, whether of others or yourself. So long as you do, you not only devote valuable energy —and as the dungeon keeper, part of your consciousness — to doing so, but you prevent yourself from moving forward in various aspects of your life. Once you cease using it in this way, however, your mind becomes freed and so do you. At that, you gain greater peace and that part of your consciousness becomes available for more productive use.

Then everything you express will be imbued with joy, love, compassion and the serenity of one who *is* neutral and at peace. You will enjoy the beauty and excellence in your own nature and in that of everyone else and you will be able to surge ahead, toward manifesting your highest qualities and fulfilling any purpose for which you have been born.

A place of honour

In the realms of your subconscious, there is a place to which you welcome all whom you honour for their greatness, excellence, wisdom, compassion, friendship, love or inner beauty. Among those who are there can be people living now or who have passed on, people you know well or had encountered fleetingly, people who have made important contributions to your life or to whom you just feel grateful for something small.

There may be people from the spiritual realm, vaguely familiar to you; and others you do not recognise, but who, in your subconscious memory, have been significant in your life. Among them, too, there may even be your pets.

There may also be people you have released from the 'dungeon of your mind' and who manifest aspects of nature that you respect. This is a place of neutrality and love, devoid of anger, recrimination or resentment.

In particular, there is someone manifesting the highest aspects of his or her nature, fresh, natural and in perfect health ... someone who looks very much like you.

To forgive is to be free.

And now to higher things

CHAPTER ELEVEN

The Non-physical You

You are not your body, nor your brain. You are a thinking, observing intelligence, enveloped in an electromagnetic system, to which your body is connected by a flexible 'cord'.

According to Sylvan & Muldoon in their classic *Projection of the Astral Body*, we disengage from our physical bodies when we sleep, sometimes experienced as 'flying dreams', finding ourselves high up, or falling from great heights.

When out of our bodies, we can travel limitless distances, to strange and beautiful places in non-physical dimensions, converse with others who are also out of their bodies and even with those who no longer possess bodies.

When suffering from early stages of dementia, one of my brothers, a distinguished physician, told me that although his vocabulary was normally restricted, in his dreams he found himself engaged in perfectly lucid conversation with seemingly very important people.

When in this state, we can also receive information as to

future events. This would explain that familiar 'déjà vu' experience, meaning 'already seen', which is of having dreamed of being somewhere, or of having had conversations, in advance of their actual occurrence … or even, possibly, of having *rehearsed* the events beforehand.

The electromagnetic system vibrates at a very much higher frequency than that of physical matter. For this reason, when detached from our bodies, we can pass *through* solid matter, such as walls, as if it were not there; which, in that dimension, it is not.

Throughout the electromagnetic system are said to be generators producing this energy. Known in the Indian tradition as 'chakras', meaning 'wheels' (because to people who see them, they appear to spin) seven of the main ones are located at the base of the spine, the solar plexus, spleen, heart, throat, brow and crown of the head.

In dim light, most of us can see at least a thin layer of blue-grey energy close to the surface of the body. Through a device invented by Russian scientists Valentina and Semyan Kirlian in the 1960s, this energy can readily be photographed around the hands.

Gifted people (and probably animals) can see coloured fields of energy, referred to as 'auras', around the body; the colours varying according to the frequencies at which the energy vibrates. Depending upon our mental and emotional activities, these fields are visible as much as several metres beyond the body, though the energy itself is likely to extend immeasurably further, partly according to our subconscious *intentions*.

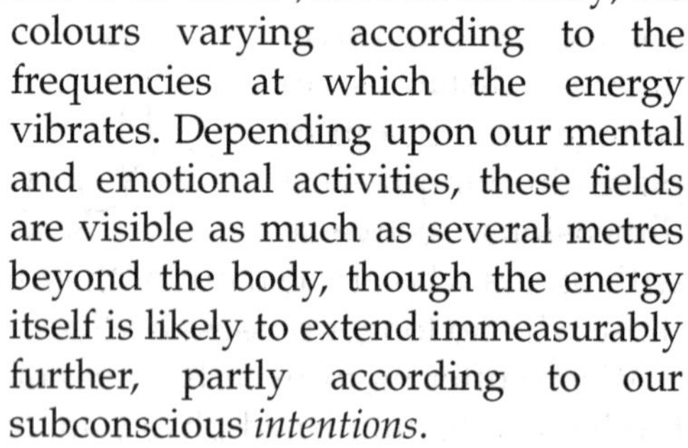

It is this energy that so-called 'healers' can transfer to those suffering from ailments, by placing their hands just over the ailing areas to enhance the immune processes. This is an ability that everyone has to some degree. Hence, mothers instinctively placing their soothing hands on their children and even our doing so to ourselves when in pain. The elderly can also enjoy the input of this energy.

When active, our 'generators' appear to stimulate their corresponding physical organs and vice versa. Hence those familiar sensations as 'butterflies' in the stomach, 'aching', 'heavy' and 'broken' heart, 'down-heartedness', 'heart on fire', 'heart-felt gratitude', the heart 'opening' and 'speaking from the heart'. They also appear to respond to vibrations, which would explain our emotional responses to musical instruments and even to others' energies. Hence that feeling of warmth when we are close to those to whom we feel in some way compatible; and that 'drained' feeling when close to those we do not, or in crowded environments, such as department stores.

Mental direction of energies

Many people have demonstrated their ability to direct their energies to objects at a distance. In the 1960s, for instance, Russian farmer Ninel Kulinga was famous for being able to cause small objects to move across a table; while scientist Karl Nikolaiev showed he could turn on a light bulb via an electronic device from a distance of several metres. In more recent times, Israeli born Uri Geller (one of a number of people in the world) has demonstrated his ability to cause metal objects to bend and a compass needle to rotate.

The effects of love, gratitude and appreciation

In his book, *The Isaiah Effect**, author Gregg Braden refers to a number of highly significant experiments on DNA that indicate the existence of some form of communication between living cells, irrespective of the distance.

In one experiment, samples of the DNA of donors' white blood cells were placed into chambers, where changes in *electrical activity* could be measured. Fifty miles away, the same donors were then shown video clips that aroused extremes of emotion in them, registered as peaks and troughs. At those identical moments, each of the donors' DNA exhibited the same extremes.

In another experiment, samples of DNA were placed in containers, where changes in their *forms* could be observed. Vials of this DNA were then given to a number of researchers, each of whom had been trained to generate and 'feel' different emotions. According to the emotions that they felt, the shapes of the DNA in the chambers were seen to alter. When they felt gratitude, love and appreciation, for instance, the DNA relaxed and the strands unwound and became elongated. When they felt feelings of anger, fear, frustration or stress, the DNA became taut and some of their *codes* even switched off. When the researchers then changed their feelings to love, gratitude and appreciation again, the DNA unwound and the codes switched on, once more.

This process of feeling loving and appreciative emotions was subsequently tested on a number of HIV-positive patients, with the result that their resistance to the deleterious effects of their conditions was enhanced to extraordinary degrees ... invaluable information for everyone of us, even in good health.

*Published by *Hay House*

Mental communication

We are in fact submerged in an ocean of thought waves. The degrees to which we are affected by and affect one another with our *subconscious intentions*, therefore, should not be underestimated.

In other experiments it has been found that when people wilfully direct thoughts to others some distance away (known as 'telepathy') the recipients' pulse rates and blood pressure increase. When we say people are talking about us when our ears are 'burning', therefore, this may well have some basis in fact.

When you think of others, you direct energy to them, affecting them in subtle ways according to the intentions behind your thoughts. In wishing them well, for instance, perhaps known as 'blessing', you send them 'loving' or 'healing' energy, probably from your heart centre. Hence that reference to our hearts 'going out' to others.

Accordingly, when you are attuned to others in any way — whether emotionally, spiritually or intellectually — you subconsciously exchange thoughts with them, not unlike radios attuned on the same waveband. This would explain close friends and family repeatedly coming out with the same remarks, or telephoning one another, at the same times.

Animal communication

Between higher animals, some form of mental communication almost certainly occurs. It is well known that pets (which integrate their consciousness with that of their owners) are sensitive to their owners' health and moods, sense when they are coming home and even have healing effects that we do not fully understand.

I am frequently convinced, through a diversity of situations, that I have mental communication with my two cats. One of my cats, for instance, used never to sleep on my bed. Every night, however, following my having undergone some medical tests (and before the results were even known to the laboratory) it slept on my bed, at my feet. Many readers can doubtless recount similar experiences.

On another occasion, when one of them was lying across the papers on which I was working, I mused to myself as to how I loved them equally, each for its own totally different nature and how parents can love their children equally, for the same reason. At *that* moment, the other cat jumped onto my desk and sat beside the first!

I recall the charming account of a dog, jumping up to snatch a piece of fish from beside the kitchen stove, where the owner was frying fish and taking it back to the cat in the next room. I have also seen a video of a duck at a French lakeside, feeding pieces of bread to fish as they popped their heads out of the water, one after another.

Spiritual communication

In ancient times, people known as 'seers' and 'prophets', were renowned for their abilities to communicate with 'spiritual beings'. Nowadays, such people, variously known as 'clairvoyants' 'mediums', 'sensitives' and 'psychics', are to be found in every walk of life. In fact, we all have this ability and use it to some degree, even if subconsciously. Exactly how this occurs is little understood, though it is thought that the information is conveyed on very low frequency energies.

This should not be so surprising. Countless energies are reaching us from the universe. Ultra-violet and infra-red, visible to birds and insects, are two. Electromagnetic energy, transmitted by radios is another. Since these energies are absorbed by radios, it is reasonable to infer that they are also absorbed by the nerve cells of our brains, even though we are unaware of it.

There is another form of energy that affects us, which may be described as 'pressure energy', because, rather than being absorbed by our cells, it *impacts* upon them. Since this energy affects our eardrums, it must reasonably also affect the nerve cells of our brains, without our necessarily being aware of it. Dolphins and whales are five times more sensitive to this form of energy than we, which may make them that much more responsive than we, to whatever information it conveys.

What this all means is that just as we can fine-tune radios to pick up transmissions from unknown places on the planet, we should not rule out the possibility of our being able to fine-tune certain areas of our brains, to access information from unknown sources in the universe. Don't be too quick to dismiss this. After all, not so many years ago, the prospect of hearing voices over the radio, or seeing live images on television screens (and cell phones) was inconceivable. It only became a question of tuning in to the respective frequencies of energy.

Altered states of consciousness

Given that mental communication occurs among ourselves without our being aware of it, the question is as to whether it also occurs between ourselves and those in non-physical dimensions or indeed, more advanced civilisations in the universe with information or advice that could raise the consciousness of our own. If it does, of course, the problem may not be so much in receiving that information or advice, as recognising it as such. Even a scientist will disregard information of a scientific nature, if he or she is closed to the possibilities of receiving it from any such source. Jung and Einstein were two who were both open and receptive to it.

Receptivity is determined by one's state of consciousness, or the frequencies at which the nerve cells in the brain vibrate, which can alter from one cycle per second during deep sleep, to 14 (or more) cycles during periods of alertness. When we doze, dream or meditate, for instance, they vibrate at around 5 cycles per second. Known as the 'theta' state, this is one in which mental imagery occurs and the intuition, or 'sixth sense', is at its most efficient. This is particularly so when just awakening.

Laboratory experiments have shown that when clairvoyants tune in to spiritual beings, they are partially in this state; which is also when solutions to problems, brilliant ideas, unusual information and inspiration from unknown sources tend to present themselves to us. You may notice that many of your most inspired ideas occur to you while you are bathing, shaving, making up, gardening, playing golf, relaxing at concerts, enjoying slow music, gazing unfocused into the distance and so on. Albert Einstein is reputed to have confided to his friend Carl Jung, that when he meditated, numbers appeared in his mind. His theories of relativity and of the universe as a continuum are said to have occurred to him at those times.

There is also the famous account in scientific circles, of the French scientist Friedrich Kekule of the 1890s, who had been trying to decipher the structure of the benzene molecule. One night, in a dream, the image of a snake swallowing its tail appeared to him, which transpired to resemble precisely the structure of the benzene molecule, known today as the 'Benzene Ring'.

Inspiration only necessitates having a question in one's mind, then observing whatever word or idea silently passes through the mind immediately afterwards. In this way, advice from loved ones and others of higher consciousness may also be received, as we shall see in the next chapter.

It does not automatically follow, of course, that what *seems* to be inspiration or advice, is necessarily so. This can also be a fabrication, based on wishful thinking, or erroneous beliefs that we hold. Many a crime has been committed as a result of fabrications misinterpreted as divine commands. So whereas some of what appear to be inspirations may certainly be authentic, it is important to be sufficiently sensitive to recognising whether they are, in fact, or otherwise.

The more open you are to the possibility of receiving inspiration from non-physical dimensions, particularly in your dreams, the clearer that information will become, not to mention the remarkable and sometimes 'unearthly' places you appear to visit.

SUMMARY

- ♣ You are enveloped in an electromagnetic system, which produces fields of energy.
- ♣ Your fields of energy are sensitive to those of others and to those emanating from other sources in the universe.
- ♣ When you sleep, you leave your body and travel to distant places.
- ♣ By being receptive, you can receive inspiration from those of higher consciousness, both consciously and in your dreams.
- ♣ Conversations in your dreams can be with people of both physical and non-physical form, including higher intelligences in other dimensions.

Allow your intuitive abilities to help you in your life.
Each day, for a moment,
feel love, gratitude or appreciation for something.

CHAPTER TWELVE

In the Non-physical Dimension

We are not human beings living a spiritual existence.
We are spiritual beings living a human existence.

Terry Tillman

What is 'life'? Is it a purposeless period, with nothing more to do than eat, sleep, achieve, procreate, endure hardships, enjoy pleasure and bide our time until we die? And when we die, will that be the end? Do we then cease to exist forever?

What of all those who die through accident, violence, war, famine and other disasters? Have they lost their opportunities to live, forever? Did all the eminent people throughout time, attain their achievements for nothing? What of our own achievements? Will they be of no consequence to us after we die?

On the other hand, if we go somewhere afterwards, will that mean the end of our troubles? If so, why bother to cultivate a higher nature now? Why not be totally selfish instead and go about our lives without concern for others?

From where do the great scientific and musical inspirations come; and the inspirations for all the magnificent cathedrals and temples in the world? From where does the knowledge of those child-geniuses come, whose abilities are so extraordinary as to defy rational explanation? Why do we find golden light so beautiful and ethereal music so moving? What do we mean when we describe places as 'heavenly' and faces as 'angelic'? Do these evoke some distant awareness in us of somewhere we can we sense, but cannot quite recall?

What follows may provide some answers to these and many other questions. It may also open your mind to the possibility of the indefinite continuation of life and to the importance to all of us of making the best possible use of the time available to us in our present physical existences.

There is of course no proof that anything that follows here is either true, or completely accurate. But, as I say in the Introduction, maintaining an open mind will enable you to reach out to undiscovered riches, which may lie beyond the current horizons of your mind.

'Near death' and 'past life' experiences

People throughout the world have consistently given similar accounts of what are described as 'near-death' experiences, under general anaesthetic during surgery, or immediately following accidents. They have described being separated from their physical bodies, looking down on the operating tables, or scenes of accident and hearing the conversations of those present. Many have recalled being at the end of a tunnel in brilliant light, where they were told that it was 'not yet time' and that they had to return. Some have even seen indescribably beautiful places that convinced them that 'death', as we understand it, cannot be possible.

There have also been innumerable accounts, under hypnosis, both by adults and children, of what seem to be former lifetimes. Some have spoken in foreign languages of which they had no current knowledge, while others have described the moments leading up to their deaths.

Descriptions of homes, villages and countries, which they had never visited during their current lives, have subsequently been investigated and verified in detail.

Such extensive evidence of 'near death' and 'past life' experiences suggests that we do go somewhere after we die, that we have had repeated physical lifetimes with different personalities and that between those lifetimes, full consciousness continues in some non-physical, or 'spiritual', dimension.

This may explain the empathy some of us have with particular cultures and biblical or historical accounts, the fascination archaeologists and historians have for ancient civilisations and that others have for so-called 'science fiction'. It may also explain the irrational phobias and allergies with which some people suffer, particularly in early childhood, children's dreams, gifted children turning up in the most unlikely families and much, much more.

Where we 'go'

As mentioned in Chapter One, according to the evidence I have received from my parents and brothers, we do not cease to exist at the conclusions of our physical lives, nor do we rest in eternal sleep, whether in cemeteries or anywhere else. As we become detached from our physical bodies, I am told, we find ourselves in the presence of people in 'spirit' form — usually family, or others with whom we have links of love — who escort us to their dimension.

Some people who have just died, readily accept this new reality. Others, not realising this has in fact occurred, may think they are still physically alive, or are dreaming and, under the care of 'helpers', gradually adjust to their new condition. Children, too, are cared for lovingly until they have adjusted.

This scenario may seem hard to believe at first. However, through clairvoyants, I myself am satisfied that members of my family and friends are fully alive and active in another dimension. My father has spoken of initially meeting previous friends and also of being able to be in more than one place at the same time. My mother has spoken of no longer being burdened with a body that would not do what she wanted. One of my brothers has spoken of exploring the various energies there. The other has spoken of studying the peoples of historical times. He has also spoken of continuing to practise medicine in that dimension and that he is studying the energies that relate to disease.

When appearing to clairvoyants, those in 'spirit' form normally present themselves in good health ... which of course they are; no longer having physical bodies. To each other, however, they appear as energy, radiating light of varying intensities, according to their development and consciousness.

Our current vocabulary is of course quite inadequate to describe what occurs in dimensions other than the physical one with which we are currently familiar. However, after many years of interest in this subject, I can offer the following, though at best, only a fragment of what perhaps occurs 'there'. Indeed, any attempt to gain an accurate perspective of that dimension must be like peeping through a pinhole, into a vast realm of existence, beyond our comprehension or imagination. Our perspectives must also inevitably be distorted by our individual realities and how we conceptualise abstract information ... as would life in a metropolis, to people who have only known existence in the depths of some remote jungle.

Life in other dimensions

There are countless other dimensions. Those dimensions coincide with one another, though they do not conflict, because they manifest at different frequencies, or bands of vibration. So each dimension 'exists' only to those manifesting within the same band of vibration.

This may be compared to radio waves, which are broadcast everywhere, but only manifest through receivers attuned to the same frequencies. You may be co-existing with intelligent beings in other dimensions right now, yet be unaware of their existence, except when your consciousness becomes attuned fleetingly with theirs.

Love, a channel of communication

Although we and they exist in different dimensions, the love we feel creates what may be imagined as 'channels of communication'; the greater the love, the stronger the communication. Accordingly, when there are strong shifts in our emotions, they are instantly aware of these.

Those with whom we have this communication are often around us, even though we may be unaware of their presence. They might encourage us in our endeavours and take pride and pleasure in our achievements, even more than they may have done when they were in their physical states.

Their consciousness is not as limited as our own, because there are no physical constraints through which to do so. They are therefore more aware of what is occurring around us than we are. Based on the directions we have chosen, they can also see further into our future than we; as we might, when looking down at the traffic on the roads from an aeroplane, for instance.

They can see, hear and sense what we and those involved with us are doing and thinking and, though we may be unaware of it, may try to advise us through very subtle inspiration. They may also give us advice through clairvoyants where we request it, provided this does not conflict with any 'universal law', or benefits we might gain through finding our own solutions to particular problems.

They are not 'all knowing', however. Those who have recently left their physical bodies will continue to hold some of their old opinions ... even political and religious. So their advice might be based on those opinions. Yet, it is possible for them to seek guidance from more advanced beings, who can see even further than they, both into our likely future and, of course, theirs.

They are aware of what we think about them, even when we sleep. However, we can also express to them consciously, aloud or by thought, whatever we wish we had told them when they were here physically. What we express aloud may be clearer than by thought, because the images in our minds are then more clearly defined.

If our thoughts are cluttered with heavy emotion, as is normally the case just after those we love have passed, we create densities of atmosphere, which they need to penetrate, or 'ride', like waves. So the calmer our emotions are, the clearer the communication. This gives us an interesting picture of the effects of thought and emotion in that dimension.

They respond to our love and wishes of well-being. Rather than being dismissed as 'dead-and-buried', as many people imagine, they desire to remain in contact, certainly during their earlier periods in that dimension. They feel elated through our elation, sad through our sorrow, disturbed through our turmoil, at peace through our peace and, I am told, they 'dance' on our laughter. For this reason, rather than mourn for them interminably after their passing, expressing our love and appreciation for what they have contributed to our lives would be more welcome.

Hence, in your dreams, you may find yourself engaged in conversation with them, which may explain the experience of crying or laughing in your sleep. I am also told that, initially, candlelight is helpful for them to locate us; one candle, apparently, being preferable to many.

Your guides and mentors

Among those in the non-physical dimensions, are beings of very much higher levels of consciousness, who also once existed in physical form. To those who see them, these beings radiate auras that resemble rainbows, iridescent mother-of-pearl or golden light. They also radiate vibrations, some of which can be too intense for others to bear, when very close.

Known in spiritual circles as 'guides', some of these beings elect to be our mentors, inspiring us during our lives so far as we permit this, with the moral principles manifesting in higher dimensions. We can have several such guides, according to the levels of our learning and any missions we have set ourselves.

You may sometimes have indications of the presence of guides or loved ones. When you feel low, for instance, you may feel that familiar sense of reassurance that 'everything is going to be fine', or inexplicably feel a welling up of emotion. You may even momentarily see golden lights, said to be the energy fields of those who have tuned in to you, possibly signalling their presence.

The more we encourage our life-companions to counsel

us, the more they will do so. Any such counsel will be according to what they sense we will understand and is appropriate. They may put thoughts or images into our minds, during our waking moments or while we sleep. They may even prompt us in certain directions, physically. Keep in mind, however, that we ourselves determine the courses of our learning on our life-journeys. Our guides are simply there, when we are open to receiving.

Next time you are walking in the sunshine, try this: With the sun behind you, try to walk along so that your shadow is always ahead of you. When you see how difficult this can be at times, you will have a sense of how difficult it must be for our friends to guide us ... particularly when the sun disappears behind the clouds and your shadow fades from view.

Try this too: when there is a war scene or boxing match on television, turn off the sound and watch without it. You may then gain a sense of how those of higher civilisations in the universe looking in, might see our world and despair.

Receive help and advice

You can request help or advice from your guides, loved ones and others of higher consciousness. *'I need your help/advice'* is all you need say or think, explaining what you need and your reasons. You may find the appropriate response arriving from the least expected source. Take this seriously. I speak from personal experience.

My mother once recounted an incident to me about some doves that used to visit our garden. One afternoon, my mother was praying for the success of a surgical operation that one of my brothers was about to undergo. At that moment, some of the doves filed from the garden, up some steps, across the terrace, through the morning room, into the kitchen, around the table where my mother was sitting and then filed out again. The operation was successful.

Many years ago, following a failed, six-year, legal action in which I was embroiled, I was bankrupt, my world had collapsed around me and I was at my lowest ebb. One night, when I was about to sleep, I wept and to my spiritual guardians I called out angrily, *'I can't manage alone. I need your help'*. Then I fell asleep.

A night or so later I had a dream. I was in a beautiful, cream, Arabic building. Pieces of mosaic began to fall from the domed ceiling onto the floor round about me, which I began to collect. Then some young men in traditional dish-dashes smiled at me. A few days later I received a call from the representative of a certain Sultan, inviting me to supply some valuable rugs for one of his palaces.

Requests are prayers. If you do not *genuinely* need help, you will not generate the charge necessary to energise the transmission of your request. Repeatedly reciting paragraph after paragraph of text composed by others, or vacantly declaring into the air: *'We pray for ...'*, can obviously not generate the same level of charge as that which would be generated through expressing, in just a few words, what you *truly feel*.

Although we can ask for help for ourselves, by the way, there appear to be limits to which we can do so for others. Those of higher consciousness do not, or perhaps cannot, intervene in the lives of those who do not desire it. Those needing help, apparently, must request that help for themselves. Keep in mind, too, that other spiritual beings will be watching out for their own loved ones. So don't ask for something that would be unjust to someone else. Any request you make should be just for all concerned.

Although a request can be addressed to someone in particular, I am told, this is not necessary, because according to the nature of the request, it will reach the 'appropriate ears'. Even so, visualising someone who you think might be appropriate could make it easier for you to express your request.

In the non-physical dimension, communication occurs wholly through thought, which is perceived by whoever is attuned to the same frequency. In the same way that, in the physical dimension, we attract and repel people according to the extents to which their natures correspond with our own, in the non-physical dimension, those we attract and the environments and conditions we encounter are determined by the frequencies of our vibrations. So, those we attract can range from the very primitive to the highly evolved; and the conditions, from those of disharmony and conflict, to those of harmony and beauty, according to our habitual thoughts and intentions.

I recall an occasion, when I was with a clairvoyant at the College of Psychic Studies in London, that a 'being', said to be from the Pleiades (a civilisation elsewhere in the galaxy) unexpectedly came through. The Pleiadean asked the clairvoyant to convey some information to me on the subject of directing mental energies, about which he or she was aware I had been thinking some weeks earlier.

Conditions in non-physical dimensions

In the non-physical dimensions there is no night, day or season by which time may be measured, because 'time' as we perceive it, does not exist. This can be difficult to understand, relating everything as we do to time and space. Nor does 'sleep' exist as we know it. Instead, I am told, there are variations in intensity of consciousness.

The ambiance in those dimensions ranges from darkness to brilliant light, according to one's consciousness; the higher the consciousness, the more brilliant. Those in non-physical dimensions are also said to be able to see more vivid colours than those to which we are accustomed.

Some may perhaps be equivalent to those we see refracted through a prism or diamond; others are beyond our normal visible spectrum, such as infra red and ultra violet.

Initially, there can be streets, parks, gardens and animals, according to our realities and what is foremost in our memories. There will certainly be opportunities to review our lives, teachers to convey higher forms of thinking and behaviour, environments to explore, education in a form we would understand as music, concerts, debates and yes, even political arguments. There will be others needing our help, beautiful books to be absorbed and occupations beyond our present comprehension.

So long as we intend to refine our nature, we spontaneously vibrate at increasingly high frequencies. In this way we come to resonate with those of higher consciousness, as would be the case on this physical dimension.

The more spontaneously we empathise with others, human and animal, caring out of the heartfelt desire for their needs, the higher becomes our consciousness and so the finer the frequencies at which we vibrate. The finer our 'vibratory states' are prior to leaving this physical dimension, the finer will perhaps be the conditions in the non-physical dimension into which we become integrated.

This integration would not be determined according to anyone's judgement of our 'worthiness' or 'unworthiness', but simply according to the frequencies at which we vibrate, which are impossible to fabricate. So the vibrations of those whose intentions are to betray or otherwise misuse their power over others, for instance, would simply be too coarse to integrate with those of finer vibrations and, in extreme cases, create quagmire-like states.

Our intentions cannot be fabricated, because we either do

'intend', or we do not. So no amount of self-righteousness, or mindless religious ritual before we leave this dimension, can create that integration. Nor can devoting ourselves to the service of others do so, if 'doing good' is only a contrivance to avoid acknowledging any lower patterns that exist in our nature. There is obviously a difference between behaving in 'good' ways because we wouldn't *think* of doing otherwise and doing so for the rewards we hope to reap.

Your personal advancement

Our experiences in each successive physical lifetime, it appears, are determined by the intentions with which we leave previous ones. As our intentions change, our experiences change. The changes in our advancement are therefore determined wholly according to our intentions.

Once in the non-physical dimension, we choose the courses we then take. Some of us will remain inactive for a while. Others will choose paths of investigation. Others still will choose ongoing growth and advancement. Some will choose to return to the physical dimensions in due course and others, perhaps, not.

We can remain at our current levels indefinitely if we choose, or through intending to change our nature, open the way to more advanced levels. One factor that contributes to our advancement is the degree to which we are willing to forgive. Another is the degree to which we are willing to respect 'the truth'. The less rigidly we are attached to our former opinions, or beliefs, the easier this becomes.

Only mental powers exist in the non-physical dimensions, for which reason it is easier to eradicate any undesirable patterns from our nature while anchored to the physical dimension and able to interact with others. Physical death does not eradicate these patterns for us.

As I see it, in the same way that creatures return as the same kinds of creature in successive lifetimes, when we return to this or some other physical dimension — though not necessarily with the same genders or, of course, identities — our natures become transferred to the neural pathways of our new embryos. Except where we have modified our natures in the interim periods, any patterns we possessed at the conclusions of our previous physical lifetimes, therefore, will continue in ensuing lifetimes. Eventually, when we have modified our natures sufficiently, we will not perhaps return to the same physical dimension, but to one more refined and of a higher consciousness.

According to an ancient Buddhist theory, we may repeatedly be re-born into the same groups from one lifetime to another, varying our relationships and even our cultures. If this is so, those with whom we are in some way associated this time around, may have been our relatives, close associates, or possibly even opponents in previous times.

Who knows what our relationships were with others we encounter, seemingly by chance; and how they may have diverted the courses of our lives according to some plan. Who knows what our relationships were with the friends we have today and what they will be, next time.

The consequences of previous lifetimes

There is another theory that what occurs in our current lifetimes is what we have created in former ones. As to what or how much we have in fact created, who can know? The law of cause and effect in the universe is too complex for our limited consciousness to grasp. However, it does seem likely that at least some of what we are experiencing now is what we have set up previously. If this is so, it would follow that at least some of what we experience in future lifetimes will be what we are setting up for ourselves, today.

Each time we take on new bodies, we will take with us the knowledge and experience we have acquired during and between former lifetimes. Thus equipped, we will continue our learning processes, in due course passing our accumulated knowledge and experience to our descendants, who in turn will pass it on to theirs, ad infinitum. In this way the human species will learn, refine what it has learned and evolve. In this way, too, each physical lifetime will become a springboard from which we approach both our future physical and non-physical existences.

The message: self-regulation

If the foregoing is accurate to any significant degree, the message must be that we should do all we can to refine our natures and raise our consciousness while we have the opportunities of doing so in this existence. This entails continually regulating our intentions and conduct until, rather than through any conscious effort, this self-regulation occurs so spontaneously that our natures have *actually* changed.

If we do not want to have to rectify next time around what we fail to do before we leave this time, it must be in our interests to take advantage of the opportunities afforded to us now. Not to do so, it seems to me, must be to lose out on invaluable opportunities for which we may have to wait eons of time, until the appropriate parents to whom we can be born once again, become available.

Why you were born to your parents

There are many theories as to how we come to be born to our particular parents. According to Buddhist theory, we choose our parents, because, through them, we gain the appropriate learning experiences for our ongoing advancement.

As to whether this is a conscious choice seems to me unlikely. Rather, it seems that at the points at which it is appropriate for us to return to the physical dimension, we gravitate to embryos whose genetic codes are compatible with the nature we have evolved so far ... in other words, that vibrate at compatible frequencies. This would enable free expression to the various aspects of our nature, which we can then reinforce or modify as we choose.

Your higher purpose

Why is it, within the same society, that some people hold totally opposite points of view to others of equal intelligence? Why do some relentlessly pursue their own ends at the expense of others, while others will not do so, even under tremendous pressure or temptation? Why do some care about justice, animals' feelings, global poverty, global warming, the ecology and the future of this planet, while others show total disregard for these? Why do some pursue 'the truth' with single-minded determination, while others resist it with equal determination? The answer to all these questions may be that some are responsive to the inspiration of higher-consciousness beings, prompting them to reach for their levels of consciousness.

Through being open to that inspiration, you can receive guidance, attain higher levels of consciousness, attract more of what you need, advance your life and advance the lives of others.

Like offloading ballast from a hot-air balloon, as little by little you eliminate the lower aspects of your nature, you will see the higher levels of existence for which you are reaching, in ever clearer and more brilliant perspective. As these upward shifts of consciousness occur, you will come into finer attunement with those of higher consciousness.

SUMMARY

- There are countless other dimensions, each manifesting only to those existing within its band of vibrations.
- At the conclusion of our physical lives, we exist in some non-physical dimension.
- The nature we have evolved up to those points is carried forward to our next physical lifetimes.
- We can advance to higher levels of consciousness and existence now, through altering our nature.

Attune to your higher nature

1 Find a photograph of yourself when you were one or two years old. Ask the child in the photograph:
   a) what changes in nature he or she would like you to help him or her make during this lifetime?
   b) whether he or she feels you have been doing so thus far and if so, what changes these were?
   c) whether there is more he or she wants you to help him or her change and, if so, what?
   d) Are you willing to do so?

2 Imagine, following this lifetime, going to a non-physical dimension:
   a) What conditions would you like to create around you there?
   b) What changes would you say you had made in your nature here, that enabled you to do so?
   c) What further changes or 'fine tuning' might you choose to make, next time around?

3 Visualise a planet inhabited by a highly advanced civilisation, where everyone's subconscious intentions directly affect one another and where everyone supports one another. There is no intention to betray, exploit or harm one another or any creature, everyone is advancing in consciousness and everyone is happy.
   a) Would you wish to live on such a planet?
   b) If so, could you be sure you would have no subconscious intention that might adversely affect any person or creature there?

4 Imagine you have the ability mentally to radiate and receive messages, to and from everyone on this planet.
   a) What message would you most wish to radiate?
   b) What message would you most wish to receive?

5 Imagine higher spiritual intelligences close to you at this moment.
   a) Mentally thank them for their presence.
   b) Invite them to inspire you with their wisdom.

6 When you are next in a public place, or when you next see someone who is unwell, radiate the thought: 'I wish you well'.

Be conscious of the guidance of higher Intelligences, for the benefit of yourself and the planet.

CHAPTER THIRTEEN

Reaching for Higher Consciousness

Vast as our planet may appear to us, to the universe it is but a speck among a million, billion, billion other specks ... like a glimmering speck of dust caught in a shaft of sunlight through the window. This speck existed billions of years before we arrived here and will exist for as long after we have left. Others will come to it in our places, testing their formulas for surviving, in turn vacating their places to yet others, ad infinitum.

As we have seen, life does not end simply because we no longer possess physical bodies to anchor us here. It is an endless existence, interspersed with brief periods in a physical dimension, where we can make use of the opportunities to change our nature and attain higher levels of consciousness, when we choose.

Like climbing a mountain, pitfalls and obstructions will certainly be encountered along the way. From time to time, too, we must fade from view as we ascend through the clouds, only to re-emerge beyond them, in time. And when eventually we reach the summit, we may find that it is actually a plateau, from which other mountains rise. After resting awhile and encouraged by those of higher consciousness, we might resume our evolution, toward still higher levels of consciousness and existence.

The next level for all of us, perhaps, will be in a non-physical dimension. Then, for some, it will once again be in this physical one; and for others, in a more evolved, higher-consciousness civilisation of the universe. Yet, if you choose it, a higher level of consciousness can be yours, now. With just a little effort you can reach that level, by eliminating some of the patterns of behaviour in your nature that are not in harmony with those of higher consciousness and reinforcing those that are. All you need do to achieve this is *change one switch at a time* among your neural pathways.

Acknowledging the truth is one crucial step toward achieving this. Neutralising any anger you may be harbouring is another. Caring about other humans and creatures and using your power over them justly, are others. Reciprocating with *gratitude* those who have provided you with your bridges, is another. Inspiring others with your wisdom, another.

The world needs inspirers

Perhaps you underestimate your ability to make any significant difference on this planet. But consider this arithmetic: If you inspired someone to begin raising his or her consciousness today and the two of you inspired two others tomorrow, all of whom inspired four the next day, then eight, then sixteen and so on, the consciousness of all six billion people on this planet would rise in just thirty-three days. And if it took a year at a time instead of a day, the consciousness of the entire planet would be raised in only *thirty-three years*.

There are not just a few inspired people in the world, however. There are millions ... in every country and in every walk of life, working toward this end. So, through your making the necessary changes among your neural pathways and manifesting the highest aspects of your nature along with them, now, the raising of consciousness of this planet could be accelerated beyond recognition, in your time.

Then, under the eyes of the higher civilizations of our universe, this planet would become transformed, not only into a paradise for ourselves and those who follow us, but into a beautiful oasis in the deserts of our galaxy.

You alone can make the changes among your pathways.
This lifetime is available to you to do so.
You have the ability … and you have the choice.

CHAPTER FOURTEEN

Mental Relaxation

This mental relaxation process is a simplified form of meditation, through which the neurons in the brain slow down to the theta level and physical tension becomes reduced.

The process suggested here need take only a few minutes. It is ideally performed each morning, though it can also be performed before retiring at night. If tension begins to develop at any time while you are travelling, at the dentist, hairdressers, during boring concerts, talks and so on, this process will prove helpful in reducing it.

If you retire at night with a worry on your mind, your system will tend not to be fully relaxed, but will remain in the 'fight or flight' state of tension. This process will help you sleep more restfully and may even reduce the amount of sleep you need.

This process should not feel like a duty to be performed religiously, but a pleasant experience to which to look forward. Sometimes you may not feel in the mood, or perhaps have sufficient time for it. Even so, a brief one or two minute session will always be better than none at all, as this will maintain the pattern in your brain. In time, you will find that the moment you begin this process, a sense of relaxation and peace spontaneously begins to flow through your body.

Seated comfortably, with your eyes gently closed, put any worries or problems out of your mind for a while and breathe naturally, a little more deeply than usual to begin with. As you do this, focus lightly on the various limbs and organs of your body in turn, intending them to relax and any excess charge to leave with your breath as you exhale.

Start with your DNA, feeling grateful, appreciative or loving for someone or something. Then, in turn, relax the palms of your hands, arms, shoulders and neck, then the soles of your feet and legs, working up through your body to your throat, mouth, cheeks, brow, behind your nose and your head. As thoughts pass through your mind, briefly acknowledge them, then release them.

If you have any knowledge of anatomy or physiology, by all means go into detail, even to your cellular level. If you have an ailment, direct your subtle energies to it for a few seconds, with the intention of enhancing its healing, in support of any medical treatment you may be receiving. Finally, inhale *very gently*, as if up through your spine to your brain and as you exhale, think, *'I am at peace'*. At this point, your mental state should ideally be one of quiet, peaceful awareness. Enjoy this quiet state for a moment or two.

If you cough, sneeze, or need to break off briefly to attend to something important during this process, simply slip back into it again afterwards. If there are any persistent noises, rather than irritate you, allow their vibrations to soothe you where they seem to resonate within your body. The important thing is to let your mind rest.

Playing some slow music, such as Beethoven's *Moonlight Sonata*, or the many New Age pieces available, can be very helpful at the commencement of this process, as it will help bring your neural activity down, naturally, to the slow theta frequency. (From personal experience, I would be cautious about using devices or tapes that necessitate using headphones, designed to bring about altered mental states *unnaturally*, as these can have other, undesired effects).

If you have difficulty relaxing a particular part of your body, it may be that you are generating some charge there, relating to some painful or annoying episode in your life. Independently of your brain, the neurons in your muscles (including your heart muscles) record their own responses to past situations and respond to future similar situations in the same ways. So if you feel tension somewhere, acknowledge any thought that appears, because that tension may relate to an experience or person relating to that time. Then 'release' it. Each time you do this, whatever stress you have accumulated on that account should become reduced.

Acknowledge those in the non-physical dimensions

This is a nice point momentarily to acknowledge the presence of loved ones, guides and others of higher consciousness in non-physical dimensions, even though you may be unconvinced that they are there. It can also be a good point mentally to ask for assistance or advice and to be open to receiving any replies.

Return to full wakefulness

Prolonged mental relaxation will normally bring you into an altered state of consciousness, even though you may *feel* fully awake. For this reason, you should ensure that you return to full alertness at the end of each session, by breathing deeply, stretching thoroughly and, if possible, talking. This is essential if you intend to engage in any activity requiring alertness, such as driving, cooking, using stairs, or walking in the street. If you are retiring directly to bed, however, this precaution should not be necessary.

And, when you do retire, this process will enhance the quality of that mysterious period we call 'sleep' and those expeditions into other dimensions we call 'dreams'.

There is an immense universe beyond the pinhole of light to which we have currently have access. In time, perhaps, we will see more of that immensity in all of its magnificence. Then we will be able to travel consciously to realms inhabited by those of higher consciousness, beyond our present comprehension.

To achieve this, however, we must be willing to eliminate the impediments to our manifesting the highest levels of consciousness that reside within us all, waiting to be freed.

If you would like to receive information on seminars that may be held near you, relating to subjects discussed in Chapters 1–10:

Email: LeonNorell@btconnect.com

Or write to: Leon Norell
P.O. Box 57505
Kilburn
NW6 9DS
UK

Please note, I cannot give therapeutic advice.

INDEX